CAUGHT IN THE CROSSFIRE

The story of Janina Pladek

told by

Mary Wemyss Aitchison

Christian Focus Publications

© 1995 Mary Wemyss Aitchison
ISBN 1-85792-149-6

Published by
Christian Focus Publications Ltd.
Geanies House, Fearn, Ross-shire,
IV20 1TW, Scotland, Great Britain.

Maps by Holmwood Maps and Plans
15 Newton Park, Kirkhill, Inverness IV5 7QB

Cover design by Donna Macleod
Illustration by Jane Taylor, Allied Artists.

Contents

Acknowledgements

I acknowledge with deep gratitude the generous spirit of co-operation with which Janina (Pladek) Neale has contributed in making this book possible. She showed great confidence in me when at our first meeting in 1968 she asked me to write her story.

Janina at that time lived in Scotland and I lived in South Gloucestershire, therefore our communications depended on letters and telephone calls. Unfortunately, the project had to be abandoned when in 1970 my husband suffered a severe cerebral haemorrhage and became an invalid.

I became his carer and main source of income for the family. Twenty years were to elapse before I could resume writing.

Having lost contact with Janina and believing that her story had been written, I returned to journalism. The unfinished work troubled me, however, and I made several attempts to find her. Eventually in 1989 I traced her to South Africa. Learning that her story had not been told I restarted in 1990. When in 1993, Janina and her husband returned from South Africa, the book was completed. If I have been able to convey to readers the courage, love and deep faith which Janina possesses, and the ever-loving faithfulness of God, then my prayers will have been answered.

Janina and I share the same deep concern for all children who innocently suffer, particularly the homeless and loveless. This concern has prompted the giving of royalties to the 'Y' Care Street Children Fund.

I acknowledge with heartfelt thanks the assistance given to me by my daughter, Ruth Larsen – the wife of a vicar, mother of a three year old and a busy vet. She has patiently edited my many manuscripts and encouraged me to 'get on with it'.

I express my appreciation and many thanks to my friend and neighbour in Burrelton, Moira Duthie, M.A., who so willingly undertook the laborious task of proof-reading. Their tangible and moral support eased the isolation of the lone writer.

Foreword

All of us have to face suffering at some time during our lives. We do not live in a fair world and suffering is not distributed equally. Suffering, in particular the suffering of children and the innocent, disturbs us and it is right that we should be disturbed. It seems so unfair that innocent lives should be torn and twisted by events that lie outside the control of the victim.

Yet, there is another side to suffering. We are constantly amazed at the number of people who, having faced the most appalling circumstances have been able to rise above them. It's as though they have said to themselves, 'I will not be defeated. Suffering will not destroy me. I will make something creative come from it.' In fact, when we stop to think for a moment we realise that most, if not all, creative activity emerges from some suffering. Suffering has the power to destroy. It need not destroy.

This is the story of Janina Pladek. One, who as a schoolgirl witnessed the Nazi occupation of her country. It is a story of great and terrible suffering and yet, it is not that alone. Out of the turmoil and chaos of warfare grows a compassion that extends way beyond Poland to embrace suffering people elsewhere. This is a story of courage and hope.

This story will bring hope to many and not only to those who read it. The author has donated half of all the

Royalties to Y Care's work among Street Children. In ways that could never be known to her, Janina Pladek continues to bring a message of hope to thousands.

Terry Waite
Founder Chairman - Y Care International

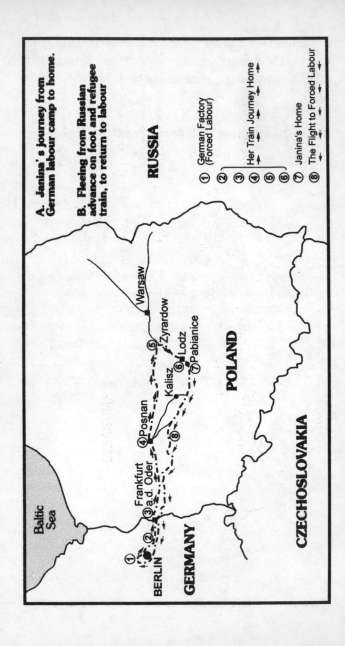

A. Janina's journey from German labour camp to home.

B. Fleeing from Russian advance on foot and refugee train, to return to labour

① German Factory (Forced Labour)

②
③
④ Her Train Journey Home
⑤
⑥

⑦ Janina's Home

⑧ The Flight to Forced Labour

RUSSIA

Baltic Sea

GERMANY

BERLIN

Frankfurt a.d. Oder

④Posnan

Kalisz

⑤Zyrardow

Warsaw

⑥Lodz

⑦Pabianice

POLAND

CZECHOSLOVAKIA

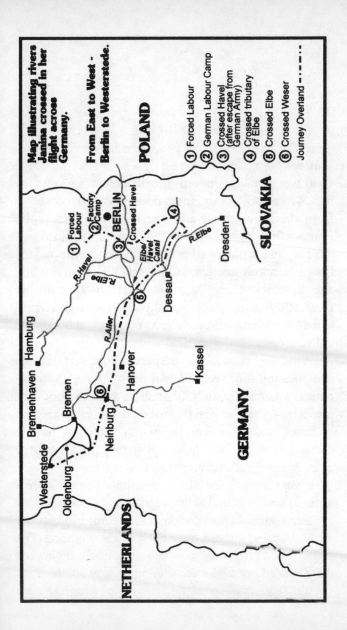

Map illustrating rivers Janina crossed in her flight across Germany.

From East to West - Berlin to Westerstede.

① Forced Labour
② German Labour Camp
③ Crossed Havel (after escape from German Army)
④ Crossed tributary of Elbe
⑤ Crossed Elbe
⑥ Crossed Weser

Journey Overland ---------

POLAND

SLOVAKIA

GERMANY

NETHERLANDS

① Forced Labour
② Factory Camp
BERLIN
③ Crossed Havel
④
⑤
⑥

Hamburg
Bremenhaven
Bremen
Westerstede
Oldenburg
Neinburg
Hanover
Kassel
Dessau
Dresden

R.Havel
R.Elbe
R.Aller
Elbe/Havel Canal
R.Elbe

Introduction

Whither goes

I was wet, clumsy, shivering, teeth chattering. With icy hands I knocked at the main door. I waited, cowering from the biting wind and torrential rain. No reply. Frantically I knocked again and again. Still no reply. Groping in the pitch darkness I made my way round the house searching and searching for another door. I found one. I knocked and knocked until my fists ached. Eventually an angry voice shouted, 'What do you want? Get away! We want some sleep. You are waking up the entire house!'

What did I want? I was desperate, cold, wet through and starving. For weeks I had been fleeing from enemies – Germans and Russians. I had no food nor protection. I had been hiding in cellars, forests, sleeping in bomb craters, swimming rivers, and now having crossed another river in face of enemy fire from both sides of the river I had reached this house.

It was the early hours of the morning. The rain lashed down. The wind howled through the trees. I was hungry and exhausted. I continued knocking until a light came on. It revealed a room full of beds – all occupied. The sight of beds filled me with a deep longing. I shouted that I would not stop knocking until I had shelter.

With shouts of swearing and cursing the front door

opened and an old man told me to be quiet and not disturb his guests. Then he looked and taking pity on me said, 'Follow me. The place is full up with guests such as yourself. I could be in serious trouble for sheltering you. All I have left is a barn attic which is full up, too, but there is straw on the floor and it will get you out of the rain.' Warning me to crouch low close to the wall so that I should not be seen he took me to the barn. Placing a ladder against the wall he knocked on a small wooden hatch under the barn roof, 'Open up!' he shouted, 'I have a young girl. Move over and let her in!' There was the sound of shuffling from inside the attic, then the hatch opened and I climbed in on to a bare floor. The roof was low – too low to stand up. I crawled over legs and boots and huddled down. The opening closed. It was pitch black!

The silence was interrupted only by snoring and coughing – incessant coughing. I sensed that the occupants were men, but what did I care? What did anyone care? We might be inanimate objects.

I started shivering and could not stop. The floorboards seemed to be shaking with me. My heart beat loud and fast and I thought it would burst. A man's voice called out, 'Here girl! You can't sit up all night. Here is a little straw. Lie down on it.' Pushing his neighbour's legs over he pulled a little straw from under himself. I took it and crouched down.

As I lay in the dark I listened to the wind whistling against the roof. It reminded me of our barn in Poland and the times as children we played among the sweet smelling hay and straw. Would I ever see my home again?

Suddenly I longed for nothing else in the world than a bath, or just a wash or just some warm water and a towel ... and home! As I fell into a disturbed sleep my mind drifted back to home ...

1

Love Repaid!
September, 1938

'The world is very beautiful ...'

Home was a farm near the village of Pabiance, about fifteen miles from the city of Lodz.

Like the others around, the farm was situated on flat land surrounded by hills. There was no large expanse of pasture or large fields. When Papa took over the farm on the death of his father the land was poor and marshy. My parents struggled for many years during which they dug and drained the land by their own efforts. Now it was producing a rich variety of crops, vegetables and fruit, which in summer made a colourful tapestry when inter-mingled with red poppies, blue cornflowers and yellow sunflowers.

The year was 1938 and harvest time, a season which generated so much feverish activity. Everyone – my family, farm-hands and neighbours – laboured day and night to reap and gather in the ripe grain whilst it was still dry, for this was the culmination of a year's work and our whole livelihood depended on it.

This year had produced a good harvest. There was now a feeling of deep satisfaction and a sense of relief. All was safely gathered in and the barns and granary were full. Although tired, dusty and covered in sweat, everyone was happy. Tomorrow we would celebrate. No matter how late it was; no matter how tired everyone felt, the preparations for tomorrow's festivities would go on.

Mama was in the kitchen and would be there baking till late into the night. Farm workers were plaiting wreaths of corn intertwined with flowers and cherries and bringing out the home-made beer and wine. But there was still tonight.

My brothers were in bed asleep snuggling under the quilts filled with goose feathers whilst, tonight, I lay on the sweet smelling hay in the loft above our chicken coop, and Papa lay outside on top of a haystack. 'How could Papa's kind heart lead to this!' I wondered.

Papa took pity on anyone in need, be it friend or stranger, and no-one was ever turned away empty-handed. He allowed the homeless or the passing stranger to sleep in the hayloft, but too often they carelessly set the hay on fire. When the insurance company finally refused to compensate him for the loss, any stranger was allowed to sleep in the warm kitchen on straw and a blanket. At harvest time there was always some grain and potatoes left in the fields. When I asked Papa, 'Why don't we gather them up?' he replied, 'In the Old Testament God told the Jews to leave the gleanings to the strangers, the widows and the poor. The poor from the village or the nearby town will come and glean the fields.'

And so they did; but soon they came not only to glean but to steal the vegetables, fruit and chickens.

The raids were so well organised that Papa was

unable to continue with the financial loss. So guarding the orchards and chicken runs became necessary.

Eugene and I had been brought up from an early age to help on the farm. I was twelve years of age and considered old enough to take my turn keeping vigil all night in the loft and listening for any intruders.

Afraid and lonely lying in the dark I was comforted knowing that Papa was close by. As I watched the stars through an opening in the roof I wondered if God really knew about me and was looking after us now.

It was a quiet, still night. Suddenly I heard the stirring of trees, but there was no wind! Could it be robbers? I shouted 'Papa'! Immediately there were shouts of anger, stones thrown, scuffling, running and then all was quiet.

Papa called me down and I went into the house and to bed.

Next morning, with Eugene and Felix, I viewed with dismay the trees, once laden with fruit, now bare. The thieves had removed part of the high protective fence and silently entering the orchard had stripped every tree. Only when greed drove them to get the fruit from the top branches by shaking the trees were they heard and disturbed.

The incident did not mar the Thanksgiving. How we celebrated it that year! Everyone had made a special effort. All the women and children were dressed in national costume. There was, however, a passion and fervour in the singing and dancing that disturbed me. Occasionally the faces of the men and women looked tense and haunted and I overheard talk, of 'the fate of Czechoslovakia', 'Hitler', 'If only Marshal Pilsudski were alive!' Reassuring optimistic voices were heard: 'It will not happen to us'; 'We cannot be betrayed again!'; 'We are strong and free!'

Soon refugees arrived from Czechoslovakia and the storm clouds gathered on our horizon.

Troubled days

Mama became pregnant and was confined to bed. Papa called me to him and said, 'You are a big girl now, Janina – the eldest. It is your duty to stay at home to care for Mama and your brothers!' I was taken aback and saw myself never returning to school and without an education becoming a farm-hand. As the weeks crept by I became more and more troubled about my schooling.

The day came when Papa sent for the midwife. She was rough and rude, calling to Mama, 'Hurry up and give birth.' Mama was very ill and Papa called us into the living room to pray.

Mama gave birth to a son who was named Theodore. But she was very ill and confined to bed for some time.

When Aunt Martha came to care for Mama and Theodore I was allowed to return to school part-time, but only after I had milked the cows and cooked the family breakfast. I returned home in the early afternoon to continue to help in the home and on the farm. To compensate for my long and continuing absence from school I was given extra homework. I had little opportunity to do it, for it was always very late when I finished my chores and I was exhausted. However hard I tried, the homework remained unfinished. I constantly apologised at the beginning of each class.

At first this was accepted but soon I received an

ultimatum from the headmaster – either I did my homework or I left school! I worked late, into the early hours
of the morning. Mama anxious about my health protested. Still the homework remained unfinished. I had
no option but to try and finish the work at school. At first
I smuggled my books into the toilet and worked there.
I knew I was breaking a strict rule and would be
punished.

Eventually I was discovered by the duty teacher. She
was lenient. I was severely reprimanded and made to
promise never to do so again. I did my homework during
school lessons, and was not found out.

This deception led me to question my honesty and
justify my actions as a Christian. It gave me a greater
understanding of others' problems and I was less willing to judge others.

'I heard a voice calling'

Brought up by parents who had been evangelists it was
natural for me as a child to accept their ways without
question. I regularly attended church and Sunday School.
In time, however, Sunday School became boring. I
joined the adults in church but that was even more
boring. However, I loved the old saintly preacher and
out of respect for him, I tried hard to follow his sermons.
But he used so many words and phrases I could not
understand, so I gave up.

Every year a Christian convention was held at which
my family took an active part. Although I refused to
accompany Mama to the evening services I was curious
about the new evangelist and went to hear him when he
addressed the Sunday School. His preaching was so

urgent and inspiring I listened attentively. The lesson was from Isaiah 53:4-6: 'He took up our infirmities and carried our sorrows ... we all like sheep have gone astray ...'. The evangelist took as an example the habits of sheep. A sheep is harmless. It has a way of wandering from one juicy tuft of grass to another until it is sometimes completely lost. Unlike a horse or dog it does not have the ability to find its way back by instinct or scent. It remains lost until found by the shepherd. I realised that my sin was my wandering away from God and being interested in my own desires. I needed to repent, and I did.

After a period of preparation I was baptised. The elation I felt at my conversion suddenly waned, and my desire to do good went into reverse. I got into trouble at school. I began to become aware of the lure of the world. It was as if someone else possessed me, destroying both my faith in and love for God. I went to the local cinema with boys and joined my cousin and other boys practising football on a Sunday, behaviour which was frowned upon in the Baptist faith. In time, however, I realised that something was lacking in my life. I was drifting away from my faith and rebelling against the 'Do nots' of the Baptist religion which seemed to be restricting my freedom. But I was not happy.

One Sunday, whilst reading a children's newspaper under my favourite apple tree, I became engrossed in an article about a girl called Hannah, the daughter of missionaries in Africa.

Hannah loved the African children and was deeply touched by the sufferings inflicted on the sick by the practices of the witch doctor. For instance, to cure a sick child he burned holes into the child's body through which 'the evil spirit' could escape. Hannah dedicated her life to teaching the people about the love and power of the God who did not wish additional suffering to be inflicted on sick people. Unfortunately, she caught a fever, died and was buried in Africa.

The story distressed me. How could a God of love allow such a thing to happen? I sobbed my heart out. Suddenly I heard a voice calling me by name and asking me why I was doubting God. It urged me to go and do the work of Hannah. I sat bolt upright and looked round the garden but could see no-one. Realising with awe that God was speaking to my heart I vowed, there and then, never to question God and his love, and renewed my promise to serve him. This incident helped me to behave and I concentrated on my studies.

I told Papa about my calling and asked his opinion. He smiled and said he would think it over.

In time Papa talked to me about full-time service and asked me to read 1 Corinthians 14:34-35 – the Scripture passages where Paul forbids women to speak to a congregation. We discussed this at length but I felt that I had to make up my own mind. Taking the Bible I sat under the apple tree. The Bible opened at the Book of Joel. My eyes fell on chapter 2 verses 28 and 29: *'Your sons and daughters will proclaim my message ... at that time I will pour out my Spirit even on servants, both men and women.'* I was astonished! I had not known that these words were in the Old Testament. Being a 'doubting Thomas' I decided it was merely coincidence and flicked over the pages at random. My eyes fell on even more incredible and amazing words.

They were contained in the book of Habakkuk, a book yet unknown to me, in chapter 2, verses 2 and 3: *'It is not yet time for it to come true: But ...what I show you will come true ...it may seem slow in coming but wait for it ... it will certainly take place and it will not be delayed.'*

I gasped. The prophesy was so relevant to my longing. This time I did not doubt and was comforted. It seemed, however, that God was rebuking me for doubting him. I knew now that I must trust God and wait, letting him lead me a step at a time.

Visiting evangelists were always welcome at our home and I looked forward especially to seeing an outstanding and famous preacher named Gerhardt, who came from Prussia. He was tall and fair, with large blue eyes. He had a kindly face and had a habit of saying 'Hallelujah' in such a way you knew he meant it. I watched him as he entered our house, bending low to avoid hitting his head on the doorway. His eyes fell on me and he touched my long blonde hair, saying, 'Hello, melinka, and what are you going to be when you grow up?' When I replied, 'An evangelist or missionary!', he replied, 'Oh, how wonderful! God bless you child.' I was encouraged that this learned man did not seem surprised or express doubt at such an ambition.

I loved and admired my father and tried hard to emulate him. When he expressed disappointment in me for refusing to join the Pentecostal church with him, I felt lonely and unloved.

My bedroom had no light and I grew afraid when going to bed during the dark winter nights. When kneeling by my bed saying my prayers, my imagination would run riot and I was terrified of something gripping me from under the bed. In time, however, I was so desperate to feel the presence of the Holy Spirit, that I forgot this childish phobia and wrestled in prayer to God beseeching him to fill my emptiness. Eventually a wonderful peace fell over me. I climbed into bed and I fell into a deep sleep. When I awoke next morning the world seemed different. I was full of joy. God was good. I wanted to tell everyone about God and his love. I loved the world. I loved the people I met. I wanted them to know Christ as I now knew him and I had to restrain myself from stopping everyone. I saw needy people everywhere and I wanted to help!

Then our world was shattered!

2

Forebodings
1939-1943

'When our world fell apart'

It was 1939. Everything was going well. The hard work
to drain and cultivate the land was a success. After years
struggling to pay off debts and make the farm profitable
Papa and Mama could now enjoy the benefits. When his
father died Papa and his brother Theo inherited the
farm. Uncle Theo and his family disliked both living in
the country and farm work, and eventually they left,
Papa buying their share of the property.

The top floor of the farmhouse was let rent free to a
family on condition that they laboured on the farm. The
tenants, unfortunately, were dirty and lazy. They neither worked nor paid rent and neglected the flat until it
was filthy and rat-infested. Now they had gone too.
Mama and Papa cleaned and decorated the flat and we
now awaited new tenants.

There was a feeling of great expectation and a
brighter future. Papa now owned the farm. The house
and outbuildings had electricity. The herd of cattle had
increased and calves were being sold. There was the
promise of a rich harvest. With so many blessings, who
could believe talk of war!

Beginning like a small dark shadow over our lives, rumours of war were whispered until they grew in loudness and intensity, looming and threatening over the land and deafening the people's pleas of 'It cannot be!'

Mama refused to accept any suggestion of war. She had already experienced the horrors of the First World War when she and her family had to leave their land and farm in the Ukraine. 'A tragedy like that surely cannot happen twice in a person's lifetime!' she insisted. 'Have I not already lost my home and my family and been uprooted from my homeland?'

One night when gazing up at the sky hoping to see shooting stars, which I loved to do, I saw what I can only describe as flying saucers. I was gripped with fear as I watched them twirling and rotating across the sky in an arrow-like formation in groups of four. They were aglow with light resembling the setting sun as it sinks into the horizon. I called to Mama and Papa, and speechless they watched the spectacle too. As the flying objects disappeared into the horizon, I experienced for the first time a fear which seemed to gnaw into my heart and paralyse me.

When neighbours talked of seeing this strange phenomenon too, Mama began to accept the possibility of another catastrophe.

Dealing with a demon
I always looked forward to being invited to my friend Trishka's farm. We were both learning to play the piano and enjoyed practising together. Her father had recently retired from being choirmaster at our chapel after twenty years service.

Without warning he became ill. His doctor could find nothing physically wrong with him and diagnosed him as dying of starvation caused by a phobia which prevented him swallowing. My friend's father, Jan, insisted that he could not swallow. As soon as he put food into his mouth something held him by the throat, choking him. In time he isolated himself in a room and continued to refuse food, becoming weaker and weaker until he was bedridden. Friends who visited him spoke of an evil presence and never returned. 'If Jan is choking, it can only be the devil himself who is doing it', they all said in agreement. It all sounded so unbelievable to me.

One day when visiting Trishka, her mother, Marie, asked if I would visit Jan as he wanted to see me. She warned me, 'When you go into the room you will feel a presence there just as everyone else has done, and I do too. It is terrible, as if Satan himself is there! Will you dare to go in?' she asked. Marie assured me that Jan was not insane, but had lost faith in himself and believed that he was a hypocrite; that his twenty years service as a choirmaster had been for his own glory and not for God's. Now he believed that the devil possessed him and that he was going to hell. I assured Marie that I would not be afraid and believed what she said, adding that even the devil had to go when Jesus commanded him to do so.

I entered the room and stopped suddenly, terrified! Something – unseen, but powerful and threatening, filled the room with a demoniacal presence. In an inexplicable way I felt separated from Jan by an impenetrable but invisible barrier. Jan lay in bed pale, emaciated, with the haunted look of a soul in torment.

Recognising me he beckoned, calling out, 'The devil is strangling me. I am dying and going to Hell, to Hell! I am beyond salvation!'

My heart cried out for him, but I said as calmly as I could, 'Why do you think you are going to Hell?'

Jan replied, 'Because I am a hypocrite. All I have done has been for self-glory and not for the Master. For twenty years I have done this and now the devil has got me. I am going to Hell!'

I assured him, 'Jesus has died for *all* our sins, even the sins of hypocrisy. He wants to forgive you, too.'

At first Jan just stared at me, then he said, 'For hypocrites too?'

I reassured him that Jesus shed his blood for every sin. As I spoke a great calm fell on the room, and the silence brought Marie in to see what was happening. I went over to Jan's bedside and prayed a prayer of repentance and gave thanks for God's sacrifice of his Son. Peace came to Jan.

When Jan died Marie came to see me. She said, 'That day when you came to see Jan the atmosphere in the room changed to peace and love. When Jan died he was at peace.'

Forebodings of war continued to be talked about. Superstitions, because of the fear they create in the mind, can cause untimely accidents and disasters, but sometimes a healthy fear can save lives. The flying saucers phenomena is still being mocked or investigated, but the fact that I saw them prepared me for the events of war and I took action to learn about emergency situations. Papa taught us how to extinguish fires and make our escape should this become necessary.

Flying saucers were soon replaced by enemy aircraft and a life of death and terror began.

Betrayed by the beast

The outbreak of war was very unreal to my brothers and me. As the enemy aircraft flew overhead we watched spellbound, until bombs fell mercilessly around us and we raced to the fields, Mama carrying little Theo. We lay flat and motionless in furrows until Papa with the help of the farm-hands dug and built shelters. The attacks intensified and continued day and night.

At first our farm escaped damage whilst the village was almost erased. Houses were bombed or burned down. The dead and injured lay everywhere. I remember during an air raid seeing a mother, with a young baby in her arms, clinging in sheer panic to a Polish soldier, and both being torn open by gunfire. The baby was left crying on the ground.

All too soon the German planes took control of the skies. Planes zoomed low and no-one was safe outdoors or indoors. The Polish army commandeered our farm and dug trenches. Some soldiers in sheer desperation and panic attacked enemy aircraft with their only weapon – a rifle, dying fruitlessly in the vain attempt to fight back.

Papa was often absent from the farm helping neighbours bury their dead or extinguish fires that were destroying homes and farms. Cows mooed plaintively in the fields for there was no-one to milk them.

Neighbours and farm-hands were, without warning, conscripted into our forces. We did not have a radio, but Aunt Martha whose son had built one with headphones brought us news, and sometimes we were allowed to listen. My brothers and I found it exciting. It was only when our Polish defences crumbled with such tragic consequences that the war became real to us.

The early and sudden collapse of the Polish defences left everyone grief-stricken and bewildered.

Feeling secure by the non-aggression pact with Germany and more cordial relations with our neighbours, Poland, concentrating on its new found freedom, was not prepared for war with a powerful enemy such as Germany. The German-Russian pact in August tragically aggravated our situation and we found ourselves fighting the powerful beasts alone.

With Eugene and Felix I stood by the roadside near our farm and watched spellbound the 'cavalcade' of our brave soldiers, horse-drawn carts, gun carriages, and lorries, continually moving west taking men from the villages with them as newly recruited soldiers.

Day after day, night after night, the cavalry and horse-drawn guncarts clattered and rumbled through the cobbled village streets. Soldiers, who had hidden in our fields and walked aimlessly in and out of the house and farm buildings, silently and almost unnoticed withdrew. We were bewildered. As children we had images of soldiers standing boldly upright and fighting bravely – even to the death – defending our people and land; but our soldiers were lost in a world unknown to us – no order, no spirit; just running or hiding from an enemy as yet unseen, except from the air.

Suddenly all was quiet, as if the world stood still. The army was gone, taking Papa's best horse. There was, momentarily, a strange sense of relief, just as if an unpleasant chapter in our lives had closed. It was good to have the house and farm to ourselves, but the silence which accompanied the withdrawal – no shooting, no shouting of panic orders, no frantic activity, no air attacks – was unnerving and eerie, and numbed us with its sense of impending doom. We quickly realised how defenceless we were with no army to protect us. We were in a kind of 'Everyman's land' with a lawlessness – no order or protection – and no-one had any idea of where this would lead.

Some people were motivated by self-preservation; some by emotions stirred up by hatred at a time when the country was almost driven out of its wits by dread of what lay ahead; and some, fuelled by memories of a cruel past when Poland was under the domination of Russia, Austria and Germany, were guilty of the most heinous crimes. Cruel atrocities were committed under the cover of darkness. My brothers and I lay in bed shivering with terror listening to the cries of agony from villagers who, trying to escape across our fields, were caught and murdered often by their own neighbours. Afraid that he might be suspected of being a spy my cousin Joseph hid his radio.

My favourite cousin Janek fell victim of this madness. He taught at a local school. He loved his country and volunteered for the army. Janek was an orphan and during his student and school vacations he worked on our farm and stayed with us. He did this to financially support his mentally handicapped sister to whom he was devoted.

It was the summer of 1939 when we last saw him and as he said goodbye to me he hugged me closely and affectionately. Tears sprang into his eyes and he said sadly, 'War is going to start, Nina, and I feel I shall not see you again!' Janek was tortured and beaten. His fingers and toes were hammered flat. His writhing body was roped to a lorry and dragged along until he was dead. A terrible end to a brave, kind, Christian young man by, it was alleged, his own countrymen inflamed to kill by a disturbed psychopathic villager.

The German attack and defeat of our country was so swift that it was impossible to organise an evacuation of the young, sick, disabled and elderly. In fact, no-one had time to escape. In advance of the German invasion refugees, mostly Jews, moved through the village causing confusion and panic and tragedy.

The fear and panic of the Jewish people was understandable. They were mostly refugees fleeing from the Hitler regime; but their action stirred up emotions amongst an insecure and frightened nation, and unhappily caused tragic incidents.

I was on my way to visit Aunt Martha when I was confronted by a group of Jewish refugees gesticulating and waving their fists in the air whilst warning the villagers about the terrors of the Hitler regime and his conspirators. They shouted, 'Watch out. Hitler has got his conspirators among you. They are everywhere. You must murder them before the German army comes and they murder you all!' I was stunned and ran home terrified. Intuition warned me that this could mean our family. Germany was a Protestant nation. Poland was Roman Catholic. Our family were Baptists. Mama and Papa were immigrants from the Ukraine. There was no knowing what a mob, especially of illiterate people, whipped up into a frenzy would do.

Our Baptist chapel was plundered. Bibles and songbooks torn up and burned. Soon we heard of atrocities to our members. Some suffered a cruel death; their bodies completely mutilated by knives. We were terrified. Would we be next? Papa thought otherwise, for he felt he had no enemies. But a faithful farm worker broke the news to him. We, too, had our appointed murderers. Two men were overheard in the village boasting about killing the Pladek family. Later they were seen, prior to the deed, consuming large quantities of vodka in the village inn. In a drunken stupor they began waving their knives in the air. A quarrel broke out between the men. They started to fight, and in the brawl both were fatally wounded. Miraculously our lives were saved.

I could not believe that our country folk could be so cruel, but the incident taught me how quickly hatred and revenge can possess one's soul and the innocent suffer. Self-preservation at such times led some to take wrong and cruel actions with, too often, tragic and far-reaching consequences.

The invasion

It was a beautiful Sunday morning. The sun shone from a cloudless blue sky. A perfect day to walk to church, but since the hostilities began all churches were closed. No shops were open, and no businesses were operating. Everyone had to survive as best one could. We were fortunate living on a farm. We had milk and farm produce and my parents baked our own bread. Nothing could be sold, but we helped others in need.

It was a Polish tradition on a Sunday for forecourts of houses to be strewn with white sand collected from the river bank and then brushed into decorative patterns to make the place clean and festive in preparation for the Lord's Day. This Sunday was to be no exception.

Mama and I were brushing the yard and had stopped for a moment to gaze at the beauty of the countryside and admire the golden corn glistening in the sun and gently waving in the warm breeze. It would be a rich harvest this year. Our attention was drawn to movement on the horizon. Spread out in a long line and silhouetted against the sky, soldiers and tanks seemed to cover every inch of the land.

On they came, tanks and men flattening the corn. Mama gasped in disbelief, 'They are coming unhindered and trampling down our grain. A year's labour and next year's provision for the village being mercilessly destroyed. Once again there is blood on the harvest!' Grief-stricken and rooted to the spot we watched, strangely fascinated, for it was so unreal, and then recovering our senses ran to break the news to the family.

'Soldaten hier!' (Soldiers here) yelled a German soldier as he entered the farmyard. We shook our heads, but despite every denial every nook, cranny and corner of the house, outbuildings and farmyard were all meticulously searched. Hay and straw was stabbed with bayonets – anywhere, anything which may hide someone. This swift and unexpected invasion occupied our land without any resistance. Our harvest fields were destroyed and the buildings damaged by offensive rifle fire, but we were unharmed.

My brothers and I watched with curiosity as German reinforcements passed the farm. The German soldiers were friendly to this newly invaded nation and offered cigarettes to the villagers and sweets to the children. Our first reaction to this was that perhaps the Hitler regime was not so bad, and Papa, uplifted, recalled how he was treated with respect by the Germans when as a Polish officer he was captured in the 1914-18 war and held as a prisoner-of-war.

Much was to happen to change all our minds!

The occupation

The German army took over the running of our district immediately and I soon realised the tragedy of war. Our farmhouse was only slightly damaged, but most of the village homes were devastated and there were many casualties – civilians, soldiers and animals.

The Germans issued strict orders. Everyone was to help clear the potholed roads, demolish unsafe buildings, clear rubble and bury the dead. Because Papa spoke fluent German he was enlisted to pass on the orders and make sure that the work was carried out.

I ventured out into the village and was horrified at what I witnessed. Houses and roads lay in ruins. In stunned silence I watched the burial of the charred bodies of soldiers, villagers and animals. Some villagers were trying to bury a dead horse. It was large and swollen – like a balloon – and covered in flies. The animal had obviously suffered and died from many gunshot wounds and its stomach lay open. I felt sick. I shuddered. As soon as I was spotted by the villagers I was ordered to 'Clear off! This is no sight for a child.

There is also a grave danger of contamination and disease.' There were many dead animals and the stench, intensified by the warm and sunny weather, was nauseating and suffocating.

I walked away, dazed and bewildered at the sight of so much devastation and horror. Many shops either destroyed by fire or shelling had been plundered, for strewn in the streets were articles of clothing, sweet jars, tins and empty cartons. 'Who at a time of common suffering could do such a thing?' I wondered. Grain stores and shop cellars were looted and emptied. For weeks there was no food or bread available in the shops.

Our farm, like many others, had its own supply of flour, and Mama usually baked once a week – big round loaves made from rye flour, as well as cakes and biscuits. During this crisis people without any food shared our supply and very quickly it ran out. We had an old coffee grinder and I recall Papa grinding down some rye husks and Mama trying to bake bread with it. It was bitter and horrible with so many husks in it.

Eventually a kind of order was restored in the village and the shops were opened. Food, of course, was rationed. There was no sugar or flour but each family was allowed half of a small loaf of brown bread. Each day there were endless queues but there was never enough loaves to meet the demand. Many people with young families to feed returned home distraught.

Desperation led men to plunder the shops, although terrible punishment or death was meted out when caught. Identity cards and ration cards were issued and a curfew imposed. No one was allowed out after six o'clock in the evening. Papa was again enlisted and given the responsibility of issuing the identity and ration cards, and our house commandeered as the reception centre. From 9 am until curfew the people queued, had their fingerprints taken and signed their cards. A German soldier looked on, making sure that everything was carried out according to their orders.

The Germans insisted on law and order and enlisted anyone who could help them. Papa was not willing to yield allegiance to Hitler, whom he looked upon as the 'prophesied beast of the Book of Revelation', and he was wary of the Nazi regime's cunning and treachery. He wanted, however, to be able to help the villagers and felt that by co-operating with the issue of identity cards and food coupons he could do so. I had never been biased by religion, colour or nationality, but I was inwardly terrified of the Nazis and tried not to show it.

I had not expected the German army to recruit Poles and was shocked to find some of our most patriotic villagers wearing a German uniform which had a swastika on the sleeve. We feared resistance to this development from the less co-operative Poles. There was no open rebellion for this was not possible. But we knew of pockets of underground resistance were encouraged by the fact that the Polish government and army were in exile in Britain, under the heroic leadership of General Sikorski.

The Germans were brutal, even when punishing minor offences. One of our neighbours was beaten, tortured and hanged for only stealing a goose to feed his starving family. It was all so cruel and unjust.

When I saw one of our fine young neighbours dragging himself along on crutches, having been beaten up by the Nazis, I was ashamed that our house had been used for registration purposes and sorry that Papa, because of his knowledge and education, had to come in contact with the German authorities. I was deeply troubled. I was too young to understand it all, but very slowly I began to realise that we were all living a double life.

Shock after shock, blow after blow, the terrible truth of our domination by the Nazis was brought home to us. Our young men were forced to join the German forces. Schoolteachers, public and civil servants, anyone who had been or was employed by the Polish authorities, were imprisoned. News of children being abducted was secretly passed around, and distressed relatives came to Papa for help. Papa would go to the German authorities and plead for them and sometimes he was successful. When the local headmaster was imprisoned Papa was able to obtain his release. He was asked more and more to act as mediator and advocate. He never refused a plea for help and we could see that he was getting himself into a very dangerous situation. The German authorities began to suspect him, and some villagers misunderstood his motives and questioned his loyalty to them. But because of his knowledge of languages Papa was needed by both sides.

Then another blow fell. Orders were issued banning all church worship, and we grew fearful of the reaction by the people. Churches were closed, plundered and put to other use by the Germans. Chapels were pulled down. Anything relating to Christianity had to be taken down and destroyed, even in the homes where by order photos of Hitler had to be displayed. The Germans demanded that all crosses, statues and shrines be pulled down and destroyed by the Polish people. Papa refused and so did many others. Perhaps because Papa was not a young man and disabled by rheumatism caused by his years in a German prisoner of war camp, or because he was needed to maintain liaison between the Germans and the villagers, whatever reason, he was not forced to undertake the demolition work. A close friend forced to remove a heavy iron cross was killed when the cross slipped and fell, crushing him to death.

Life became more perilous. All Jews were ordered to wear a yellow star on their clothing and, tragically, were banished from the village and towns into ghettos and concentration camps. Jews and non-Jews disappeared and villagers were found shot. There were whispered reports of people being sent to a concentration camp in Lodz. Young people (mostly schoolchildren) were taken by force from their families to work in labour camps in Germany. A school friend of mine, Christina, to avoid being abducted, went into hiding which meant living without a ration card. She was discovered by the Germans and driven away. When her clothing was returned to her parents they knew she was dead.

Papa helps Jews and other needy people

Abductions began to take place during the night when people were indoors obeying the curfew. Papa still insisted in doing all he could to help people whilst there was time to do so. He enlisted the help of friends or contacts he had made when selling his farm produce before the outbreak of war. Several of them lived in the city of Lodz where Jewish ghettos and a concentration camp had been set up. Under the German occupation all deliveries by farmers were under strict supervision. Permits for travelling, delivering and carrying goods were necessary.

By some secret means, I never discovered how, Papa received information and appeals for help from those in the ghettos. It was necessary for anyone travelling through Lodz to pass through the ghettos which were enclosed by high barbed wire fences and gates guarded by armed German soldiers. Only permit holders were allowed through. They could not, however, stop in the ghetto or talk to any of the detainees. (In fact it was even forbidden to talk to other villagers in the street during the occupation.)

Nothing would prevent my father from trying to help anyone in need and when he knew he had to pass through the ghettos he saw it as an opportunity to help the starving internees. He hid sacks of potatoes and bread in the bottom of his cart. As he moved through, turning a corner out of sight of the guards, he would slow down without actually stopping the cart to allow Jews to swiftly remove the sacks. It was a carefully prearranged plan and a brave, humane but dangerous act. Papa would return home distraught at the sufferings he witnessed but could not prevent. Jews lived in appalling and crowded conditions, several families to a room without any heating, comfort or sanitation. The hunger and poverty was terrible.

Each time Papa set off, the sweat would begin to pour down his face, but knowing that the lives of the Jews depended on getting food he continued to take the risk. Mama was sick with worry and my brothers and I stayed close to her until Papa returned. We knew that if he was discovered we would be sent to a concentration camp and Papa would be executed.

Not only did we live with this awful fear but Father's kindness became known and soon there was a constant stream of mothers, fathers and old people pleading for food for their children or sick relatives. Papa could not turn them away. He was under orders to provide the German personnel with provisions and to disobey could have cost us our lives. In order to help our own people he altered the diet for the cattle and fowls. Small potatoes which were fed to the animals were given to the needy, and the animals were fed on clover and any root vegetables. To allay suspicion, and provide a reason for so many people calling at the farm, Papa would ask the able-bodied to do some farm work in lieu of payment. Some were too ill and weak to do so, but they were given potatoes, vegetables and, before they left, some milk and a slice of bread. It was my job to weigh out the potatoes and I shall never forget the eager grasping of the bag and the look of deep gratitude.

During the potato harvest we were never short of workers. I overheard Papa arranging with a worker to repay him with his lunch, tea and a sack of potatoes for a day's labour. The man happily agreed. Later another man came and accepted the same terms. After lunch a man came seeking work. He was exhausted, hungry and dispirited. Papa asked Mama to give the man some bread and milk, then offered him work doing some weeding in the garden after he had finished eating. When it came to allocating the potatoes I was told to give each man the same. The man who came last was surprised and happy. He went off calling his thanks. I asked Papa, 'Wasn't it unjust to give all the men the same amount?' and he replied, 'It is fair. They all needed it and their families depended on the potatoes. After all the first received his lunch and a sack of potatoes, and the last one who only asked for food, was worn out and discouraged before he started, yet he worked like a slave. He deserved the same reward.' I was reminded of the parable of the workers in the vineyard (Matthew 20) and the hiring of servants when each received the same amount.

Continuing my education

Like all schoolchildren I was naive about the future. All schools were closed by order of the German authorities and I became anxious about my schooling. I was determined to reach matriculation, for I was sure that God wanted me for full-time service. Being a woman I had no hope at this time of becoming an ordained minister. My only hope was to become a medical missionary. It saddened me that I dare not openly express my Christian beliefs. Knowing that God was aware of my love for him, however, comforted me and I stubbornly resolved to use whatever ingenuity I could to serve him.

Schools where only the Polish language had been taught remained closed by order of the German authorities, but German schools set up to indoctrinate children into Hitler's dogma were gradually opened. Parents were forced to send their children, under the threat that if they did not their children would be taken from them and sent away, often to German labour camps.

I returned to school and soon became aware of the

change. There were pictures of Hitler everywhere. Our own Polish professor had been imprisoned and other teachers were missing too. The Polish language was forbidden and removed from the school curriculum. We felt concerned and uneasy, but became absorbed in our studies. My parents feared that I should be misled into Nazi doctrines. They did not suspect that my allegiance was a pretence to deceive the German authorities into allowing me to study at the college in Lodz.

Eugene refused to attend school. Felix, only ten years old, was punished for refusing to accept the Hitler indoctrination, and later he would not attend school. Papa was worried. There were several visits to the farm by the Nazis, threatening him that his sons would be taken away if he did not discipline them according to their laws. Against his own convictions he gave Felix a hiding in front of the Nazis, rather than have him taken away and never see him again.

The authorities pestered my father to make his sons attend a weekly meeting of the Hitler youth, but he managed to convince them that the boys were needed on the farm. Eventually Eugene and Felix worked on the farm full-time.

I was older than my brothers and realised that if I did not convince the authorities of my allegiance to Hitler I could be sent to a labour camp at any time. The fact that I helped my father on the farm had delayed my going, but time was quickly running out. When a German professor was appointed to our school we realised we had to be extremely careful. To allay any suspicions about my loyalty I began attending meetings in the village. They were not well attended and the leader gave up, asking me to take her place. She tried to persuade me by saying that I would receive an official appointment from the German authorities as a leader. The meetings were seldom supervised by the Germans and it was obvious to me that I would be able to do more or less what I pleased under the guise of the authorities. Instead of listening I would be able to do something, and I saw the opportunity to serve God. I accepted the leadership, but not the official recognition.

At school I made friends with a Russian girl. We were both keen scholars and studied together. I felt I could trust her and confided in her that I was a Christian – but how naive I was. I became aware of a change in the Professor's attitude to me. One day he questioned me in front of the class on my religious beliefs. Most of my classmates knew I was a Christian, but that I must not admit it. The prompt interruption by a school friend saved me. She put her hand up and said, 'Sir, do you know Pladek holds girls' meetings in her village!' The professor turned to me and asked, 'Is that so?' When I replied, 'Yes,' he said, 'Well that is different!' I was never questioned again, and in time received my scholarship to the Lyceum in Lodz.

My parents found me cheap lodgings in the home of a middle-aged spinster. I had to provide my own meals and went daily for a bowl of soup and a bread roll to a cafe near the college. This was my only meal.

I began to feel safe hidden away, as it were, in my lodgings, studying until late into the night. I had no money for heating and would study until my hands froze and my brain seemed to numb. I had nothing to eat or drink as I could not afford it, but occasionally when at the cafe I treated myself to a glass of Polish beer with my soup or, as a great treat, an ice-cream.

I was an ardent patriot and loved the stories of our nation's heroes and heroines, especially of Chopin, Paderewski, Pilzudski and Marie Curie. I wanted to emulate Marie (Sklodowska) Curie who endured such poverty and hunger to become the world famous scientist, when, along with her husband Pierre, she discovered radium. Her endurance and dedication inspired me to study in spite of my hunger and hardship.

I looked forward to my occasional visits home, for the atmosphere in the college was very tense and disciplined by the German authorities. Some of the students just disappeared and there were times when I did not think I would be allowed to finish the course. Examination time arrived, however, and I rejoiced at passing and attaining honours. I looked forward eagerly to returning home and telling my parents.

As soon as we had our results we were asked to report to the authorities and with only enough time to collect a few necessities we were bundled into a truck bound for Germany and forced labour.

3

Forced Labour
June 1943- January 1945

Blood, Sweat and Tears

The Nazis' domination over our nation was cold, ruthless and completely lacking in any respect or love for fellow human beings, be they Jews, Gentiles, young or old. With a brutality which seared into our young hearts we were marched from school, manhandled by the armed guards and pushed into a covered truck. Villagers looked on, helpless to do anything to stop our abduction.

As we drove on through the city I was heartbroken and wondered: Where are we going?, What fate awaits us?, Who will tell our parents that we have been abducted? We were not allowed to talk to each other and could only communicate our fears through our eyes. My pride, anger at such humiliating treatment, and fear of what lay ahead prevented me from breaking down into tears, but some girls became hysterical calling for their Mama or Papa. I cradled a girl in each arm, shielding them from the guards' abuse and threatened retaliation if they did not stop whimpering.

On and on into the dusk and through the night we travelled without stopping. The trucks were driven with such recklessness that we were thrown about like loose baggage. Some of the girls suffered from travel sickness and our pleas for comfort stops were ignored.

Shafts of daylight were penetrating cracks in the covered truck as the convoy slowed down on to what seemed to be a rough country track. After a short distance it came to a halt and we were ordered out. In the grey dawn we could see the outline of a large turreted building resembling a monastery. High walls surrounded it. Men and women in German army uniforms took charge of us and we were marshalled into a large hall.

Tired, frightened and hungry – hungry for kindness as well as food – we were brusquely ordered to stand to attention. Our names were checked and the few belongings which we had brought with us were inspected and some items confiscated. I thanked God that we did not have a clothing or body inspection for I had hidden my Bible in my bodice. We were grouped into work teams of twelve girls, and marched off to our sleeping quarters. The rooms had bare rough wooden floors and rows of wooden bunks, each with a straw mattress and a straw pillow. We were ordered to claim a bunk, with strict orders that the mattress and pillow must be kept neatly in shape. Untidiness would be punished. There were no other furnishings or facilities in the rooms and our few belongings had to lie on our bunk.

With no time to rest we were given a slice of black bread and water and then marched off to begin work on the neighbouring farms. It was about 7 am.

The farmer provided us with a midday meal of bread and jacket potatoes, and how we looked forward to it. At the end of the day we returned to the monastery, where still under supervision, we continued to work, cleaning the rooms and building, weeding the garden or labouring in the vegetable plots. I was homesick and fell into my bunk exhausted, longing for home and hoping that my family could find out where I was and that I was alive.

My thoughts turned to Eugene, my eldest brother. Where was he since he was abducted by the Germans? What had become of him? I prayed that the Germans would treat him well. Eugene was tall, blond and well built – the type the Nazi wanted for their Arian race – and I hoped that this would go in his favour. I prayed to God to protect him and return him safely to his family.

We knew it would be hard and that we would be expected to be subservient to our captors, but for a group of young girls abducted from school and home without warning, the regime was without mercy. Awakened before dawn we assembled in the hall and, scantily clad, were ordered to run round the compound several times. After only enough time to swill in cold water and put on our clothes we were marched to the farm where we worked all day under supervision.

The farmer's wife seemed to trust me and sometimes she would give me a snack, making me promise not to tell anyone. One day, she confided in me that she had been disciplined by our guard for allowing me to work in bare feet when my feet became so badly blistered and bruised by the wooden clogs issued to us. Handing me a piece of bread she warned me not to upset the guards, or tell anyone about our conversation.

I was used to farm work and quickly adjusted to the routine, but I grew more afraid of the attitude of the guard towards me. She was a strange woman, tall, with cropped fair hair and steel blue eyes. She never relaxed or smiled. It was as if she loathed the work she was doing and released her feelings on us. Her dislike of me was obvious and she frequently found reasons to abuse or punish me.

We knew that it was forbidden to practise or talk about Christianity. I was not openly rebellious, for I knew the penalty was death, but I found it difficult to abandon lifelong habits. I found myself bowing my head before eating. Another time I knelt by my bunk to pray. I felt the guard knew, for her animosity towards me grew worse and I sensed her watching me closely.

One day she asked me to go to her room for a box of matches. I entered the room and was immediately confronted by her guard dog, a Rottweiler, a savage brute. Trying to appear unafraid I talked to the dog as I cautiously walked towards the shelf where the matches lay. He sat watching me intensely, baring his teeth. I picked up the matches. The dog charged. His teeth narrowly missed my throat, biting into my shoulder and tearing my clothes. I almost fell, but recovering stood upright. The dog charged again, and as I tried to dodge him he bit into my arm. I freed myself and moved away. A battle of wits began! I prayed hard, and mustering all the strength and authority I could, I commanded the dog to 'sit'. It remained motionless but each time I made the slightest move it prepared to charge.

Continuing to command the dog to 'sit', I carefully and very slowly edged towards the door. Fortunately the door opened into the room. Slowly, trying hard not to betray any movement, I felt for the handle. After what seemed an eternity my hand touched it. I grasped the handle, tore open the door and shot behind it. With a terrifying growl the dog charged and the power of its thrust closed the door with a bang. Shaking and near fainting I returned to the room where we had been working and found it deserted.

Later, my companion told me that all the girls had been ordered to another room. When, at last, the girls returned they pretended not to notice my condition, my torn clothes or bleeding arm and shoulder. I was in a state of shock and near collapse. The wounds remained painful for a long time and as a result of not being treated the scars still remain. I tried as best I could to repair my only clothing. The woman guard ignored me, even when I presented her with the box of matches and the blood was oozing from my wounds. Had she hoped, I wondered, that the dog would kill me?

On our return to the monastery we passed through the farmer's orchard. I loved orchards and would gaze up at the trees thinking of my beloved apple tree at home where I read for hours in its shade. It was late autumn and the apples had been picked, but on the tallest tree, hanging from its top branch, was a large red apple. The storms and wind had stripped the tree of its leaves and any remaining fruit, but this one apple had survived. Each time I walked through the orchard I would watch the apple swaying in the wind and hope that it would fall at a time when I could pick it up. It was so long since I had tasted one. The apple, however, remained. I watched it every day until an affinity developed between us. I decided that this apple belonged to me. There were over fifty other girls and staff but no-one seemed to notice it. Perhaps they were too tired and low in spirits to gaze up at the tree tops and notice an apple! The apple became my communicator and confidante and we exchanged such dreams and longings! It reminded me of home, and the trees in our own orchard. Every day I waited for the apple to fall. The days passed and still it stayed as if permanently fixed to the branch.

A story Mama told me came into my mind. A young girl was dying of pneumonia. It was autumn and she lay watching the falling leaves of a vine which grew outside her window. One evening when her sister entered the room to draw the curtains she noticed the invalid counting the remaining leaves. 'When the last leaf falls I shall die!' she murmured. An artist who lived in the flat below heard of this, and he took his brush that very night and painted a vine leaf on the girl's window. The days passed. The painted leaf remained and the girl grew stronger and lived.

Suddenly I no longer wanted the apple to fall. It would signify its demise! I resolved to climb the tree and bring the apple down. It was a dangerous feat, a challenge but I would do it. I waited until all the girls were asleep, and all was quiet, and crept out unnoticed. My eyes grew accustomed to the dark. Cautiously I climbed the tree reaching the top branch, but I could not reach the apple. I shook the branch vigorously. The apple fell and I caught it. I climbed down and looked at it for some time tenderly smoothing its skin. This one apple had symbolised love, challenge and life to me. I did not want to eat it, but there was no other way to keep my escapade a secret – and I was hungry!

Sent to Berlin

Overhearing the guards discussing the transfer of some of the girl workers I felt instinctively that I would be one of them, and so it was to be.

With no time to say goodbye to the remaining girls we were ordered into a covered army truck, and after travelling several hours we stopped at what appeared to be the suburbs of a large city. We entered a large encampment of wooden huts enclosed by high fencing and barbed wire and guarded by armed soldiers. Adjacent to the camp was a large factory emitting acrid smells. As we alighted aircraft flew overhead. We threw ourselves to the ground as bombs exploded nearby and shrapnel fell around us. The noise, fire and smoke; the shouting, running and confusion was terrifying. Not even during Germany's invasion of Poland was there such massive destruction and air power. Although frightened out of our wits we were uplifted knowing the Allies were near. Seeing Germany now being destroyed, and our ruthless masters cringing and frightened gave us hope that we would soon be liberated. In spite of the suffering we still had to endure, that flame of liberation kept us going.

It was 1944 and we were in the outskirts of Berlin. To keep their factories working the Germans had invented an apparatus which used gas to generate electricity. It was our task to operate the machines and keep them running smoothly. We were replacing Russian prisoners of war mercilessly shot before the Russian army advanced on Berlin. Germany's situation was indeed critical when schoolgirls were replacing men.

There were twelve girls in a working team. We were issued with workmen's overalls believed to have been worn by the Russian workers. After a brief period of instruction we were sent to work, each team in a different part of the factory. Our quarters were wooden huts in which were bunks with straw mattresses. There was no heating. We had to fetch water from a cold water pump some distance from the hut. It was winter with subzero temperatures. The icy winds blew through the cracks in the huts, and we shivered and coughed from hunger and cold.

Germany's home military force was made up of retired ex-servicemen. Our guards were elderly – a 'Dad's army'. Our guard, an elderly German army officer, long past retiring age, had his living quarters adjoining our hut. He was more resigned to his country's defeat than the young Nazis who supervised us in the factory and seemed concerned with his own comfort and survival, which was a blessing for us. Conditions were more bearable in comparison with the hatred and brutality we had suffered at the monastery. There were, of course, strict regulations and threats of severe punishment if we were discovered taking it easy. Possessing or reading the Bible was strictly forbidden and any disobedience carried the penalty of death. I began to observe our guard retiring more and more to his room and taking his dog with him. After he had made his nightly inspection and returned to his room, I dared to leave my Bible open during the night in the hope that some girl would notice it, read it and be comforted. I knew the risk I was taking and prayed that I would not be discovered.

The Allies' air attacks intensified. One night when the bombing was particularly fierce a girl called Clara became hysterical and on the verge of losing her senses. Instead of running for shelter she crouched and sobbed pitifully, clutching desperately to the wooden supports of her bunk. I crept slowly forward and putting my arms around her I said quietly, 'Clara, Jesus loves you. He will protect us and you will be alright!' Slowly she lifted her head and gazed at me sadly. I knew she wanted to believe me.

I thought of Jesus dying on the cross and Mary, his mother with John, his beloved disciple, standing helpless and grief-stricken. Jesus said, 'Mary, this is your son!', and to John, 'John, this is your mother!' John took Mary home and he cared for her, and Mary comforted John. I had three brothers, but no sisters. When Mama was pregnant for the fourth time, I prayed for a sister, but the baby was a boy. I cherished Theo, but the void of not having a sister remained. As I sat alone comforting the despairing Clara, a voice seemed to say to me, 'Janina, this is your sister!' A new wonderful relationship opened up to me. I was not alone. The girl workers were my sisters, for we all belonged to the same God. The factory received a direct hit. Some girls became hysterical, lying prostrate on the ground and crying for their parents. I tried to comfort them by talking about prayer, and this helped me too.

Food was short and severely rationed. Once a week we were given a small square black loaf, a tiny piece of ersatz margarine and sometimes a small piece of ersatz cheese. Under the supervision of an officer, we had to take turns to cook the staff's vegetables. We looked forward to this for it was such a treat to taste the vegetables as they were cooking.

The guard dog belonging to the officer in charge of us was fed on boiled oatmeal. Gradually the dog refused to eat it. Not to waste this cereal I made a kind of pancake for the girls. The pancakes were foul and unpalatable but we needed the nourishment and chewed them, spitting out the chaff. The dog was tied to his kennel most of the time and looked ill. He would look at me with such pitiful eyes and when he died I was filled with remorse and guilt for not giving him some of my rations. His death, in retrospect, was merciful for soon we were to abandon the factory and flee.

The factory instructors warned us that if our machine broke down without good cause we would be suspected of sabotage, for which the punishment was death. The gas used to operate the machines was stored in tall cylinders – about six feet high. Two such cylinders were connected to each machine. There was no gauge to indicate the flow of gas entering the machine, or the amount of gas left in the cylinder. We had to learn to judge the input and control the volume of gas. The gas was kept under tremendous pressure and when the pressure was released the gas cooled. The machine was constructed to depressurise the gas, and if this happened suddenly the gas was in danger of freezing. If the opening of the cylinder was not judged accurately the gas could freeze, causing the engine to seize up. In addition, a small amount of snow would occasionally collect round the apparatus. We would tremble in fear at what could happen as the factory was so bitterly cold.

To save fuel we were not allowed to run the engine for testing purposes and this worried us, especially when we had difficulty getting it started. One day the machine would not start. We tried the starter handle. It was stiff and, despite our combined efforts and strength, it would not move. We had no alternative but to report the stoppage. We were told, 'Two mechanics will investigate the fault in the morning. There had better be a mechanical fault!' We were terrified. Adelena, my workmate, burst into tears. 'Surely there must be something wrong!' she cried. I tried to reassure her, 'We know the engine was cold. The power could not get through. We tried everything but the machine refused to start.' It was no use, Adelena could not be consoled and in my heart I was not convinced.

We decided that we would steal out of the hut after the guard had made his nightly inspection and return to the factory. We knew the risk we were taking but there was no other way. We worked on the engine and tried our best to get it to start. It warmed up and stopped. Knowing it was a matter of life or death we doggedly worked on. Suddenly, the engine started and purred. We became excited and relieved; then realised that, if the mechanics found the machine working normally we would be in serious trouble. Adelena knew I was a Christian and she begged me to pray. I told her to return to the hut and try and get some sleep. I would stay awake by the machine and pray about it.

It was obvious that there was now nothing wrong with the machine, but something had to be wrong before the mechanics arrived. I sank to my knees and prayed. I examined the machine again and my gaze fell on a tiny screw – one that we had been forbidden to touch. Desperate measures were needed, however, and I gave the screw a few turns. It moved revealing the metal underneath to be gleaming and white. The surrounding metal of the casing was rusty and brown. I could now open the cylinder and immediately a hissing could be heard. I tried to start the engine but it was dead. Relieved I crept back undetected to our sleeping quarters.

Next morning we were summoned to the factory earlier than usual and ordered to be at the machine and stand there until the mechanics arrived. The mechanics examined the machine and failed to start the engine. We were shaking with fear. I concentrated on the story of Elisha the prophet. When his enemies came to take him to prison, he prayed that God would strike his captives blind, then under false pretences he led them to his king. I prayed that God would be so gracious to us.

As the mechanics opened the cylinder head I could hear a faint hissing sound and in desperation I prayed, 'Lord, make them deaf so that they cannot hear it!' They could not have heard for they worked on for several hours until frustrated and angry they began to dismantle the apparatus. As they took it apart and placed the pieces on the bench near where we stood my heart pounded. 'Lord, make them blind!' I cried from the depths of my soul, 'For my companion's sake if not mine, so that she too will believe that you can overrule and are a living and present God!'

The mechanics failed to notice the loosened screw. The machine was quite close to where we stood and as soon as the mechanics had their backs to us I swiftly turned the screw back to its original position. The examination completed and the machine reassembled the engine was tried and it started at once. The men looked at each other in amazement – and then at us.

They muttered that the engine must have been flooded, but could not find a reason to make a complaint against us. We were given a severe reprimand, a stern warning, and then they left.

As the raids intensified we were ordered to continue working during the raids, even when the factory was hit and gas cylinders exploded destroying the building and killing some of the girl workers. Houses and buildings in the neighbourhood were hit and we were sent out to help repair homes and replace roof tiles. It was a terrifying ordeal for inexperienced schoolgirls. We would lie flat on the roof, screaming for our parents as bombs exploded around us. Our mutual suffering and terror brought us closer to each other. We came from differing backgrounds, but we had one thing in common – we were all teenagers abducted from school, lost to our families, forced to work for the enemy in the most inhuman conditions, sharing the same loneliness, hunger and suppression. Even the lazy ones began to take their share of our harsh labour. I was asked about prayer and my faith and we became united resolving to help each other.

After working for many hours replacing roof tiles on a block of flats, Adelena and I clambered down dirty, weary, dispirited, cold and hungry. When a deaconess who lived in one of the flats invited us in we were amazed and overjoyed. She allowed us to wash, gave us a cup of coffee made with water and chicory, and some biscuits. She was a petite, kindly, middle-aged lady who very soon put us at our ease. It was the first home we had been in since we left Poland.

Christmas was only a few days away and I felt

confident enough to confess that I was a Christian and that I had hoped to make biscuits for the girls' Christmas presents. She offered to pay us a visit and came on Christmas eve bringing with her some biscuits and two recorders. She played the bass one and I accompanied her on the soprano. We had not heard music since leaving home and school and we sang and wept with joy. Except for this visit Christmas day came and went as usual. I was able to keep my promise to the girls and surprised them when I produced a few biscuits.

During the occupation of Poland all our traditional festivities were banned. The last Christmas we celebrated as a family was in 1938. I lay on my bunk remembering and dreaming. It seemed a world away. A world that had vanished all too soon through evil, greed and force.

Christmas was a joyful and holy time at home in Poland. My brothers and me loved helping with the preparations, especially making the Advent wreath. Mama showed us how to intertwine branches of fir trees and holly, and then decorate them with Lametta (paper stars). When it was finished, and all the family present, we placed four candles representing the four weeks of Advent. Papa then suspended the wreath from the living room ceiling by four ribbons. A candle was lit each Sunday and we sang carols.

Mama and Papa would secretly carry the Christmas tree into the living room and decorate it. We were not allowed to see it until we had returned from the Christmas service held in our chapel. We were so excited and could not keep still as Mama struggled to wrap us up in warm coats, scarves, hats, gloves and muffs, for it was a bitterly cold evening. Papa allowed us to travel on the sleigh. It was so wonderful gliding over the glistening snow under a heaven bright with stars.

The chapel service was a family affair. Eugene and I sang with the junior choir and Felix, along with other members of the Sunday School, recited verses from the New Testament. At the close of the service each child was given a bag of sweets – a present from St. Nicholas and also a gift from our Sunday School teacher.

We returned home covered in a thick blanket of snow. After shaking it off in the outhouse we huddled round the kitchen stove, waiting for Mama and Papa to call us into the living room. Papa called, 'Come in children and see what the Christmas child has brought you!'

Oh the joy and excitement as we entered! The Christmas tree reached to the ceiling and was laden with luscious red apples, sweetmeats and small gifts. Gifts were also spread under the tree which we believed the Holy Child had brought us when we were at chapel. There was a large tray filled with sweets and biscuits which we were allowed to eat after supper.

Afterwards we visited our beloved Aunt Martha and Uncle Josef, who farmed nearby. We sat in the cosy sitting room singing carols, reciting poetry and listening to their two sons playing their violins. I played the recorder. We drank coffee and tea and ate sweets, apples and nuts. It was just wonderful sharing in the love of Christ!

On Christmas morning the entire village was rejoicing. People streamed to their church or chapel. We exchanged greetings. Peace, joy and goodwill pervaded the homes and streets and filled the very heavens. How I wished it could last forever!

I lay on my bunk shivering. The camp hut was bitterly cold and the wind sooched through the cracks, making a melancholy sound. I could hear some girl's teeth chattering with cold. The bunks creaked as we wriggled and huddled on our straw mattress trying to get enough warmth to fall asleep. No one spoke. We were all too hungry, tired and homesick as Christmas Day drew to a close.

Next day I was returning alone from repairing roofs when I noticed an elderly lady carrying a heavy suitcase. She looked ill, worn out and distressed. When I saw her place the suitcase on the pavement and walk away, I cautiously approached her and offered to carry it. She looked surprised. We were going in the same direction but her home was in the country, further on than the camp. The roads were deserted and due to the bombing there was no public transport. It was getting dark and I decided to accompany her to her home. I had a better chance of getting into the camp unobserved in darkness.

We trudged uphill until we came to a lovely cottage set in a well-tended garden. It was so unexpected. After the austerity and drabness of the labour camp, and the mounds of rubble of bombed buildings, it was indeed a delightful oasis. I could not conceal my surprise or joy. The lady thanked me for my kindness and, beginning to trust me, explained that the cottage was her summer home where she and her husband had spent many holidays. It was to have been their place of retirement but he had died suddenly. Now that she was alone and living in Berlin had become too dangerous, she had decided to go and live with relatives in the country. She was deeply distressed at leaving the cottage and garden unattended and her flowers to die.

The place was indeed beautiful. Just seeing it was a healing balm to my flagging spirits and I offered to tend to the garden. Her eyes lit up, then she looked at me somewhat disbelievingly and asked, 'How do you hope to get away from your labour camp and come out here?' I assured her that somehow, with God's help, I would get out and look after her garden. In a strange way I enjoyed taking the risk. It gave me a reason for living – a sense of worth and purpose amidst the destruction and hopelessness. I managed to steal away unnoticed several times.

The return home (January 1945)
The Allied blitz intensified. Air raid followed air raid without any respite. There was so much death and destruction around us that it was impossible to keep the factory running full-time. The German defences were crumbling, and with the Allies gaining mastery of the skies, our guards had more urgent tasks than supervising a group of teenagers. The situation was so desperate, everyone was needed and our duties became even more arduous. Rules were relaxed, however, and there was a more tolerant atmosphere. With less pressure on us we began to think of all those who were suffering as a consequence of Hitler's fanaticism, not just ourselves.

I became more and more anxious about my family. Postal communications were non-existent. The officer in charge of us had become more lenient – even fond of us, I thought – and I decided to ask him for leave of absence to visit my family. My request left him speechless. Looking at me he roared with laughter. 'Have you gone mad?' he asked, adding that there was Hell let loose all around us. Air raids continued day and night destroying buildings, roads, railways. Casualties were high. How did I hope to reach Poland? I pleaded, 'I promise I will return. You can depend on that. Have I not served you well, cooking for you, doing your laundry. Under the present crisis you do not have a superior officer to ask for permission. You can give me leave of absence!' He tried hard to persuade me to stay for my own sake, but seeing my determination he allowed me to go.

No one believed that it would be possible for me to travel – even hitchhike to Poland. Trains were few and far between, and those that did reach Berlin were commandeered by the forces.

I pushed in my pocket a piece of bread which I had saved for the journey and set off.

There was bustle, noise, panic everywhere. I walked blindly through the streets, for I did not know the city. Even if I had it was unrecognisable and almost completely flattened. It was a place of death and destruction, with its gutted buildings and mounds of rubble. Roads and streets were torn up and impassable. Between the brief lulls in the air raids people came out of shelled ruins, like rats out of a hole, dazed, screaming in terror and scavenging for food.

I found the railway station. It was desolate and frightening. There were a few civilians looking anxious and scared, with their eyes fixed towards the railway line – hoping and waiting. What trains could get through were used by the military for transporting goods or ammunition. Some soldiers stood about aimlessly. Some appeared to have lost contact with their unit; some knew not where to go, or what to do next. In this drama of lost souls I was yet another. There were, as always, the aggressive soldiers glad to see a girl around, but most were too troubled about their own survival to take notice of a dishevelled, ragged and scruffy teenager. Two soldiers approached me and questioned me. They tried to pull me against a wall. I struggled, screaming that my friends were near by and they let me go. I was now less sure of my safety and wondered how I could remain unharmed. Polish girl labourers were called 'dirty Polaks' and looked upon as subhuman by the Germans. A lone teenager was considered 'fair game'. The cat and mouse game continued but fortunately I was left unmolested.

Anything moving east would suit me and to my own amazement my prayers were answered. I was often shouted and sworn at by soldiers for attempting to travel on trains which were now reserved mainly for military use, but I ignored it all. After many hours, during which I waited, hid in waggons and travelled by way of Frankfurt and Poznan, I eventually reached Lodz. How the city had changed! The Germans were in retreat and leaving the city as fast as they could. Fear of an imminent Russian invasion was now uppermost in people's minds and already a stream of refugees was fleeing the city. It was another nightmare, seeing haunted and starving faces and the blank stare of those without hope. 'Whither goest thou?' I mused as I started my long trek home and wondered what had happened to the inmates of the concentration camp and Jewish ghettos.

Oh! the emotions, joy and tears when a lost one returns unexpectedly. My arrival was no exception. All our pain, hunger and terror was momentarily overcome and forgotten in the excitement and wonder of being together again. Blindly I had dreamt that home would be as it was when I left, but the intervening months had brought many changes. The Germans had retreated and the village was now once more in a state of 'No man's land'; this time awaiting the advance of the Russians.

Mama and Papa had aged considerably. They looked thin, tired and ill, and Papa was more disabled. The Russian invasion was now the impending threat, and they endured air attacks day and night. The farmhouse, although damaged, was still standing but the farm buildings were flattened. There were deep craters in the yard and fields, and it was pitiful to see the fertile earth, so lovingly cultivated by my parents over many years, torn up by the bombing and partially buried under the rubble of the blitzed farm buildings.

Mama prepared a meal of bread and jacket potatoes, and we had just finished when it seemed as if all Hell had been let loose. Bombs screamed and whistled down on us. We threw ourselves under the table. The entire neighbourhood seemed to light up as bomb after bomb fell and exploded around. Mercifully the living part of our house escaped damage but the rest was destroyed.

When it was safe to do so we ventured outside. The sky in the east was ablaze with light as if lit up by the fires of Hades. We knew it was only hours before the Russians arrived.

Speechless, we watched the sight of hunched, heartbroken men, women and children, trudging through the snow and ice-covered roads in a bitterly cold winter night in an attempt to escape and find peace and freedom

– but where? Their few belongings were bundled in horse-drawn or hand-drawn carts, or carried on their backs. They called to us to flee before the Russians arrived. Mama, always strong in faith and innocently believing that we would never need to leave our home, refused to join them and went to bed as usual taking young Theo with her.

Under the cover of darkness Papa made preparations. He buried some stores and clothing, should the house be destroyed and in the hope that one day we would return. He confided in me that we must be ready to leave the farm before the Russians arrived, and together we prepared bundles of food and clothing. I decided to take my bike. Still clad in my clothes and boots I lay on top of my bed ready to leave as soon as Papa called me. It was so very good to be home.

I lay awake reminiscing on our life here, thinking of my cousin Janek, his premonitions and his terrible death, and wondering if we should ever see my brother Eugene again. How sad Eugene would be to know we had to leave the home and farm he loved so much. He had entrusted the care of his beloved pigeons to the family when he was conscripted into the German army. It was such a small thing now, but I did wonder how the animals would survive. The terror of the Hitler regime was now almost over. Could the next 'prophesied' beast be Marxism under the guise of communism?

I lay thinking of my father who put into practice the ways of Christ. He was an educated and learned man who could have chosen a well-paid profession, but instead travelled the villages of the Ukraine preaching the gospel. Whilst the Nazis tore our country apart, he risked his life and that of his family to help the Jews and his own countrymen. Now he was again fleeing from godlessness and brutality, with only his faith and the love of God to protect us.

'The Jewish people will rejoice at the downfall of Hitler and his fanatics,' I thought. They were a proud race, always keeping their own identity. You could recognise them so easily in Poland. As the Bible foretold, the Jewish race though scattered would never integrate with other races. Different languages, race or colour aroused no prejudice in me. I recognised the obvious distinction between black and white or communism and Christianity; but the Jews they were distinctive. They were meant to keep their own identity. History had made them a chosen people. When they cried, 'His blood be upon us and upon our children!', sadly they had no idea what they were acclaiming and the tragedy it has brought upon the Jewish race.

Fleeing from home

When Papa told me that he was preparing to leave, he confided in me that we must try and reach the British army lines. This was our only hope. He told me that his eldest sister had fled from Russia and communism in the 1920s. She escaped to Germany and married a German and was now living in Westerstede, West Germany. If all else failed we must try to reach his sister's home. In the event of any of us becoming separated from each other, this was at least a meeting place.

I had just dropped off into a disturbed sleep when I was awakened by Papa's urgent cry, 'Wake up! Wake up! Quickly dress! We must get out now!' It was just past midnight.

Maria, our faithful maid, cried out in terror and I tried to calm her. 'Maria, Maria dear, help us pack and come with us. Please, Maria!' I pleaded. But Maria seemed to have lost her reasoning. The strain of the past war-torn years under the Nazi regime had proved too much. She could endure no more. How I loved Maria! She had loved and cherished me. Whenever I returned home from school or a visit to Aunt Martha she would embrace me and kiss me, then, falling on her knees, apologise profusely for taking the liberty. I would help her to her feet, hold her tight for a moment, telling her that there was no need to apologise, that I loved her too – and would kiss her.

Maria came from a very poor home. There were many such places in the village. Children slept under rags, were often hired out to work for their food. If they were orphans they simply existed working as cowherds or looking after the geese or pigs.

Two such orphan girls lived near the village. Although adult women they were only four feet tall and the object of ridicule and pity. On our way to school we would meet them tending the herd of geese. The birds terrified us. They were so vicious and could bite. The goosegirls would chase the geese away with a stick. I admired their courage, but was in awe of them and could not communicate with them. Perhaps it was because they were so dirty and smelly and their clothes in tatters. Or, perhaps, it was because we were all too frightened of each other. I, because of the tragedy, sorrow, hidden fears and terrors they could reveal to me; the knowledge of which I could not handle. Little did I know that the lives of the goosegirls would soon seem like paradise compared to what my own would be.

Maria, our maid, had so much love to give and devoted herself to our care. Although our home was quite humble and could be very cold in winter, Maria thought she was in heaven living with us. Now the thought of leaving the home she loved so much was too much for her. 'Please come with us, Maria. We are your family now,' I cried, but Maria didn't listen. She ran out of the house screaming and disappeared into the darkness of the surrounding fields. We could do nothing. It was so dark. I shall never forget Maria, or that moment of utter despair and helplessness when someone you love flees from your protection in a state of absolute terror into a dark abyss. I could only ask God to protect her. Maria having been subjected to such inhumane treatment during the Nazi regime was driven out of her mind by fear of living under the despotism of communist Russia.

By the dim light of a paraffin lamp we silently packed our belongings in the horse-drawn cart. It was a bitterly cold night. A biting wind whipped through our clothing. The steam of our breath froze on our eyelashes and eyebrows and our tears froze onto our cheeks. We had to avoid arousing suspicion and being seen leaving, for Papa still had his enemies. We took all our bread and also food for the horses. Papa packed all his legal documents in a wooden box.

Mama could no longer cope and sat crying in the cart, unable to even gather clothing for herself or little Theo to wear on the journey. As it was time to leave, in desperation I grabbed a warm coat for Theo and wrapped it around him. It didn't matter if clothes fitted as long as he was warm. Throwing an eiderdown and blankets over Mama and Theo we drove off into the dark countryside.

So as not to tire the horses, Felix and I had to walk alongside the cart. I took some bread in case we were separated and made off on my bike riding alongside Papa. We had only travelled a few yards when it became impossible to cycle and I had to alight and push the bike.

When we reached Pabjanice it was almost impossible to move. Not only had we to struggle through deep snow and ice, but the streets were crammed with refugees and German forces fleeing from the Russian advance. Air attacks, bombing, machine and heavy gunfire continued to disrupt our flight. As they fled for safety, in the scramble and panic many were killed or injured. It was bedlam at its bloodiest!

Reaching the city we found traffic was almost at a standstill. The Germans had altered the main road into a one-way traffic system and reserved it for their forces. The refugee traffic tried to force a way across the main road and inevitably everything and everyone came to a halt. Battling for one's own survival became the name of the game. People on foot carrying their bundles on their back or pulling sledges were more likely to get across. I told Papa that I would make my way across with the pedestrians and wait by the side of the road, and he agreed.

As I left he called after me, 'Whatever happens do not allow yourself to be caught by the communists ... whatever happens ... whatever happens.' His voice trailed away and I could hear no more. Papa had every reason to fear and distrust the Russians. His sister Janina, a dental surgeon, had been tortured to death by the communists for refusing to deny her Christian faith and betray her patients. Mama and Papa had been forced to leave their home in the Ukraine and abandon their evangelism.

Hours seemed to pass. There was no sign of the family. I grew tired and lay down in the snow against a haystack which was close to the road. I was sure my family could not miss me. I had also a good view of the road and the endless exodus of refugees. It was a pitiful sight. Wrapped in awe at the tragedy I beheld, I felt it was unreal and that I was a mere spectator of this human drama. Did I really belong to this mass of dehumanised wretches fleeing desperately from their own country after suffering starvation, suppression and terror at the hands of the Germans; and now seeking refuge in Germany, hopefully under Allied protection, to escape the terror of Stalin and the tyranny of Russian communism?

I dropped off to sleep. When I woke up the traffic was as congested and lengthy as ever. I panicked and began asking people driving carts if many had got through. People shouted at me as I stood by the roadside not to delay if I wished to save my life. Eventually someone called, 'Keep going! Your family cut across the frozen fields when the traffic was held up by an accident. Some German cars and lorries took a side road out of sheer desperation and some people followed. In panic some tried to overtake the stream of traffic and this caused more chaos and anger ending in a number of carts overturning in the ditch, scattering the people and their belongings. This caused more confusion and hold-ups. Some people, like your father, tried to assist the unfortunate ones and others just pushed on. You must come with us!' they pleaded and I joined them.

The roads covered in a thick blanket of snow, occasionally blocked by snow drifts, icy and ploughed up by military vehicles and horses' hooves, were a nightmare for carts and pedestrians. I saw no other bikes, and realised why, as I moved only inch by inch after tremendous efforts pushing mine. I made little or no progress when moving uphill. Army lorries seemed to race past me and I had to jump quickly aside as they took up all of the road which was passable. By now there was a kind of road discipline to avoid the nasty accidents which hindered progress. The refugees began to force each other to stay in line in order to keep moving.

I continued to worry about my family. Would I catch up with them? Would they perhaps lose or break a wheel going across ploughed country, or would the horses get injured? I knew that Papa was familiar with the country, for he had travelled to several Pentecostal cottage meetings in different towns and villages.

Papa's last words as he called after me, 'Whatever happens do not allow yourself to be caught by the communists!' rang in my ears as my face turned to ice by the snow and my tears. With a broken heart I struggled on.

From early childhood, Britain represented Christianity to me through the crusaders and missionaries. The British flag – the Union Jack – illustrates the Christian faith through the crosses of St. George, St. Andrew and

St. Patrick and it was like a magnet to me. Poland was again a lost nation, and the pull and urge to reach Britain became increasingly stronger. Britain and America were also fighting for our freedom. The exiled Polish army found refuge in Britain. By the help of God I would reach the British shores. Fired by this prospect I struggled on, keeping a lookout for another hold-up.

Every time there was a mishap such as a hold-up, collision or accident, the army lorries had to stop. This gave me an idea. If I could grab hold of a lorry when it was stationary and hold on when it moved I could travel more quickly.

My chance came. A lorry stopped and I raced towards it, grabbing on to its side before it moved on. Some people guessed my intention and shouted at me in abusive language, but I could not be deterred and held on. The lorry started, moved faster and faster. It drove so close to the cavalcade of horses and carts that I had to pull my bike in behind the lorry to avoid crushing into them. Travelling in this way was more strenuous and dangerous than I had anticipated. The bike leapt about as it hit the numerous potholes in the road. I had to lean forward and unable to sit on the saddle had to stand. I longed for the lorry to slow down but it sped on.

We had travelled several miles across country and as the road narrowed we approached another village. I grew alarmed at the possibility of a serious accident when moving at such speed and realised that at the first opportunity I must let go. There was every likelihood that I could topple into an oncoming lorry and be run over. Then I remembered how wise horses were. They will avoid stepping on a living creature if possible. My only hope was to throw myself in front of a horse cart and this I did!

For a moment I felt nothing. I knew I had been hit by the cart and the bike dragged with me. An oncoming lorry ran over the back wheel of my bike crushing it badly. People came rushing and bent over me. I was carried to a nearby house and a warm room. The lady of the house gave me a hot drink. It tasted so good! I was in a state of shock, feeling like a lump of bruised flesh. Someone examined me, felt my legs and found that I had no broken bones. They said it was a miracle, for the horses had run over me. I thanked God. He did care. Renewed hope surged through me. I was now convinced that God planned to bring me safely through any troubles that lay ahead, and that he was caring for my loved ones too.

My hosts were kind and concerned. They said thousands of refugees had passed by, but they could not see the point of it. Where would they flee? They preferred to die at home than out in the cold. My bike had been rendered useless and my hosts tried to dissuade me from attempting to continue. 'You cannot walk and keep up the pace to escape from the approaching Russian lines,' said the woman anxiously. Seeing I was determined to go on, however, the man said, 'Your only hope is to try and reach the nearby railway station. The last train has gone, but a cattle train is due in the station. There are endless queues of men, women and children aiming for the station, but if you leave now you could try and get on the train.' I thanked them graciously and hurried on as best I could dragging the bike with me.

I arrived at the station just as the train pulled in. As

soon as it stopped the crowds pushed, shouted and jostled in a desperate effort to find room in a waggon. People threw themselves in and lay down on their bedding or sat on their bundles or cases determined not to be moved. I threw in my bike, clambered on the waggon and helped to pull in the old, infirm and children. Soon we were crushed against each other, for no-one wanted to be left behind. To our dismay the doors, old and rusty, would not close exposing us to the gales and driving snow.

The train did not move. We grew anxious. Russian tanks could be seen in the distance. The thought of becoming trapped and fired on by the Russians terrified us. Mercifully the engine started and we moved out of the station, first slowly, then faster but every few miles we were held up when the air attacks made it too dangerous to keep moving.

Darkness fell and we huddled together trying to sleep. In the morning I considered our situation. There was not enough room in our waggon for all of us to sit at once, far less to lie down. Next to me was a mother with twin babies. The grandmother had sat nursing one all night whilst the mother had stood with the other in her arms. She was exhausted and close to breaking point.

The injustice of men squatting and lying on the floor whilst this poor mother was suffering beyond endurance outraged me. Choosing my words carefully I spoke out, 'I am addressing those who have spread themselves out to be comfortable. We might be in this truck for days, so would those who have been sitting or lying down now stand and give others who have been standing all night a chance to sit?' There was a gasp of surprise from the women. The men stared at me, and without a word changed places with those who had stood. From then on each took turns to sit down.

Without food and water our situation became grave. Each time the train halted I went with other children to gather twigs to light a small rusty iron stove some men had found. It was used to heat snow for the babies to drink. Plucking up courage and risking being left behind I walked to a nearby farm and begged for some boiled potatoes. I knew this was the staple diet of farm folk during the occupation. The farmer's wife offered me some raw potatoes. I thanked her and when I explained that we had no means of cooking them she gave me some cooked ones. I rushed back to the train and shared them with the others.

We were travelling west away from the Russian advance. Sometimes when we reached a main station Red Cross workers would bring boiled milk pudding, macaroni or similar nourishment for babies and young children only. I queued and brought the food for the children in our waggon. I had heard my parents relate stories of the First World War, and had read about its young heroes, but never did I visualise war to be as traumatic and heart-rending as this. We were a populace of complete strangers all trying to escape to freedom, hoping to survive and find a safe haven, a place of peace and love. But where and how, I wondered? To walk away from home and family for a faith, an ideal seemed the answer, but was it? I felt like a piece of flotsam being tossed mercilessly in a raging sea until thrown onto a lonely beach to be found useful or lie unwanted until it rots or is swept away again by the tide back into the ocean.

The air raids increased and the train was frequently held up. We remained stationary for hours in open countryside with no protection from the air attacks. Terror and hunger drove some people to abandon the train and flee across the fields. Others sought protection under the waggons. Most families sat together praying, whilst some cursed; women wept and babies cried. When it was dark we huddled together for warmth and protection. We tried hard to get our bodies into a resting position and also to shield ourselves from the bitter winds and driving snow. We were desperate for food and drink. Those who had food ate it secretly in the darkness. The Russian tanks were moving closer unhindered, encircling the train, blocking our escape.

A difficult choice

I realised that I no longer had any hope of finding my family and because of the desperate situation and hunger I decided to try and find my way back to the labour camp. It seemed the only way to get away from this human tragedy of despairing crowds where everyone felt the other was in the way; where you could not drink melted snow with a clear conscience; where crumbs from a crust of bread were passed secretly and eaten secretly; where some people having reached the end of their endurance, were losing their reason. Was hardness of heart the answer, I wondered, for certainly the selfish and ruthless seemed to survive? The labour camp with all its slavery, imprisonment, restrictions and coldness seemed a better alternative. Having a known destination, a goal, grew more and more attractive and even exhilarating! I surged with renewed energy! No matter how bad it was, it was infinitely better than what I was going through. I would return to Berlin, and the quicker the better!

Ignorant of the dreadful effects of the total collapse of Germany and the massive destruction by the Allied air attacks, I had underestimated the obstacles I would face. Germany could not cope with the thousands of refugees moving in the same direction as their retreating forces.

I soon caught up with a group of refugees and befriended a girl called Lisa who had also lost contact with her family on their flight from Poland. We decided to travel together as far as possible. It seemed safer to travel together than alone.

We had been walking for hours through fields and woods when we reached a main road. Weary and hungry we accepted a lift from a German officer, a trip which was to become a nightmare! Petrol was no longer available and to conserve his supply the driver switched off the engine when descending the many twisting and steep mountain roads. The Allies were advancing into Germany on all sides. Any moving vehicle was the target of fighter and bomber attacks. We had frequently to stop and run for cover.

It was late evening and dark before the car eventually parked outside a large house in a remote village. The officer ushered us in. The house was occupied by the German army. The soldiers were lying and sleeping everywhere, on the floor, on tables, in chairs, against the walls. We were apprehensive, not knowing what fate awaited us and kept close to the officer, whom we felt we could now trust. Our entry caused a sudden stir among the occupants. Desperation, anger, defeat, hunger and fear was visible in their faces. Were we to be a divertissement? A soldier advanced towards us menacingly, but with a sharp command from the officer he withdrew, muttering under his breath.

We were taken upstairs and soldiers occupying a bedroom were ordered to leave. We followed the officer, who offered us the bed saying, 'I will lie on the floor beside the bed. Anyone approaching it will have to walk over me and their punishment will be severe. Sleep well. I promise you on my honour that you will be safe!' He wrapped himself in a blanket and lay down by the bed. We were terrified at our situation and agreed to take it in turns to keep awake and warn the other if anyone approached us. But, neither of us had known the comfort of a bed for a long time, and being so exhausted we fell asleep.

We were awakened next morning by the officer. He gave us coffee and bread and urged us to be quick. We must leave as soon as possible. We were grateful to him. He had kept his promise and so far we were safe. He drove us until we were away from the immediate battlefront. We parted, knowing that each had been touched by the encounter and wished each other well. He was an enemy, and yet he had acted honourably. We wondered if, perhaps, he had daughters of our age and hoped that someone would help and protect them in similar circumstances.

When we reached Frankfurt I was in sight of a railway station so I left my companion, but only after she had joined a group of refugees travelling in her direction. How often on my journeys I had to realise sadly that meeting is the beginning of parting!

The station was congested and crowded with distraught, impatient and noisy would-be passengers – soldiers trying to reach their dispersed units, German nationals hoping to reach their families before the final blow fell, and refugees of all nationalities fleeing from the east, from labour camps, from prisons. Passenger and goods trains were filled almost before they stopped. The young and the old were vulnerable and frequently pushed aside or trampled on in the mêlée. No one was allowed to travel without a permit or pass. I had neither; nor had I any money to purchase a ticket if I could obtain a pass. Somehow I had to find another way.

I roamed the platforms with my damaged bike looking for a chance to climb into a goods waggon unnoticed. Everyone was desperate and agitated. Tempers flared. No one had time to reason. I received curses and abuse. Time and again I was sent off by the platform guards. I would not give in and continued to drag myself and the bike up the many flights of stairs connecting the platforms. I received more verbal abuse as I bumped into people with my bike. My legs ached. My efforts to hide in a goods waggon came to nothing. It was all so useless! Tired, discouraged and starving I felt doomed to die in the station. I dissolved into tears feeling that death would indeed be merciful.

In my agony I felt the comforting presence of God wrap round me. The experience was so real that I was immediately strengthened and decided to make one more effort. I dragged my broken bike up yet another flight of stairs. I could not abandon it for I still hoped to have it repaired. Suddenly, someone behind me lifted my bike! I had not heard anyone approach and turning quickly I saw a well-dressed man. He had an empty sleeve tucked neatly into his overcoat pocket. With his one arm he carried my bike. I looked up in surprise and was immediately aware of my dishevelled appearance. I was dirty and smelly. I had not washed or changed my clothing for days. My hair was matted and uncombed. The stranger smiled kindly and appeared not to notice.

'Where are you going?' he asked.

'Berlin,' I answered, 'but it is hopeless. Everyone tells me to go back to where I came from, but how can I return to Poland even if I wished? The battlefield is moving closer.' I became silent. What was the use of talking about my problem I thought.

The man looked at me with pity and said, 'Come with me. I'll get you on a train!'

As soon as I appeared on the platform the guard recognised me and shouted, 'Get off and take your bike with you!' There was certainly no place or room for a bike.

The stranger shoved the bike into the luggage waggon and escorted me to a first class compartment. It all happened so quickly I was speechless! Here I was, dirty and stenching from unwashed flesh and clothing, sitting with a distinguished gentleman surrounded by disapproving well-dressed passengers. I blushed with embarrassment.

The guard seeing what had happened was determined to have me evicted. The gentleman produced a pass and raising his voice in anger said, 'Here! Read this! It states clearly that I am entitled to travel first class accompanied by an escort free of charge, whether anyone likes it or not.' The guard, fuming and muttering under his breath, left, signalling the train to leave the platform.

I now had time to study my companion. I presumed that he was a high-ranking German officer, who, because of his injury, was allowed an escort. Miraculously he had saved me from despair and was the answer to my prayers. 'Was he perhaps a Christian?' I wondered, but dared not ask. My companion shared a sandwich with me and when I told him where I was going he was surprised that I was returning. He knew the camp and when we reached Berlin he gave me directions to it. I thanked him profusely and he wished me well. Then we parted.

It was after midnight when I reached the vicinity of the camp. I was too ashamed of my appearance to be seen by anyone and made my way to a nearby cottage. I had become friendly with the widow who lived there when repairing her roof. I knocked on the door and was welcomed in. She brought me water, soap and a towel, saying, 'You smell just like my husband did when he returned on leave from the battlefield!' She gave me some weak coffee, which was a special treat, and then I went to sleep on a couch.

Next morning I presented myself to the officer. The girls were astonished at my return, for they had not believed me when I said I would come back. I had travelled from the middle of Poland to Berlin when Europe was being torn apart both physically and spiritually. With no money and only one sandwich I had relied on God's mercy and he did not fail me.

If I had thought that I would be granted a period of rest to recuperate from my travels, I was wrong. Much had happened since I had left. The Allied bombing had been ruthlessly effective and few buildings had escaped total destruction. Preparations to evacuate the factory and camp were hastily being made.

The Allied advance into Germany plummeted the nation into a turmoil. There was a 'wailing and gnashing of teeth' as the country mourned for their dead and feared the collapse of Germany. The bombing continued relentlessly, reducing Berlin and the suburbs to rubble. There was now no resistance from the German forces. The camp personnel waited for orders, for reassurance news, but none was forthcoming.

There was a feverish activity within the camp destroying anything incriminating or of use to the enemy. Bombs and detonators were placed anywhere that would frustrate the Allies' advance – within the camp, factory, crossroads, bridges and guarded by the 'Dad's army'. Work in the factory came to a standstill and we could only wait for orders to evacuate.

I was working in the kitchens when Adelena came rushing in.

'Nina,' she called excitedly, 'Two strangers have arrived at the camp and they are asking for you. I think they are your parents.'

'It's not possible!' I cried, but rushed out to the camp gates.

My first reaction was pity for the bedraggled couple. They looked so old and grey. Was this tired, limping man really my father; the person I always visualised as a tall, strikingly handsome man?

'Nina! Nina!' I heard the cry and ran towards them.

God was truly embracing us with compassion and love as we clung to each other and wept with joy. Papa had remembered my promise to return to the camp and the description I had given of the place and its location, and decided to make a detour on the way to Westerstede to find me. Adelena had been fetching water when she noticed the stationary cart outside the camp gates.

'Cart and horses outside the camp fence?' I had queried. 'You must be dreaming!' But it was not a dream.

Mama and Papa were, of course, eager to know how I had survived the ordeal of our flight from Poland. I told them.

They could not risk delaying at the gates for long. Papa explained, 'Darling daughter, we have no passes and it is a miracle that we have got this far, but I cannot risk the lives of the family. We could be interned or sent back to Poland. Pray God that we shall see you soon and pray that all, including the horses, will survive the journey to Westerstede.'

Papa handed me my matriculation papers and 300 zloty (Polish pounds) which he had raised by selling a cow. We embraced again. The family boarded the cart, and with a crack of the whip, they were gone!

I stood sobbing my heart out whilst I watched them disappear in the gathering darkness. Our brief meeting was so sudden, unexpected and miraculous, it was like a dream with no ending, for I did not know if we would ever see each other again. I clutched the metal box Papa had given me, for I felt that in giving me it the family had left something of themselves with me.

As we were preparing to evacuate the camp I buried my matriculation papers and the money hoping that one day I would return and retrieve them. Such are the dreams of innocent youth. Somewhere near Berlin they may still lie buried.

4

The Flight
January-February 1945

Prepare To Flee!

Our guard, Captain Herman (we named him) became withdrawn. He had served in the First World War, and never lost his military and disciplined ways. He had lost the will to serve and spoke longingly of returning home to a soft bed and good food. Food, other than what was left in the camp stores, was now unobtainable. An inventory of all foodstuff was meticulously maintained. Herman, however, unknown to the other members of staff, had hoarded a store of potatoes, turnips and carrots. He had become attached to his charges and took us into his confidence. Each day we were allowed to unearth a few vegetables to eat or make soup. I was entrusted to go to the village baker and, unknown to the other guards, returned with loaves of bread which Herman shared with the girls. At Christmas time I persuaded the baker to give me biscuits for the girls' treat.

This tolerable interlude ended abruptly when orders were received to prepare to evacuate the camp. We were to be ready to assist the army in the battlefield. The news numbed us with fear.

Orders were received from the authorities that all

alcohol must be poured away before we withdrew, to prevent the Russians from confiscating it. The Russians had a reputation for heavy drinking and going out of control when drunk, which led to the plundering of homes and abuse of women. Captain Herman had a large store of beer and he had no intentions of pouring it away. He planned a farewell drinking party after dark. The girls were excited and thought it wonderful. For one night we would celebrate; have a fling; no restrictions; no punishments! After years of suppression and hardship it would be wonderful to forget our sorrows and danger. Herman insisted that everyone had to consume the beer until they were drunk! I objected. I tried to reason that our situation was too dangerous. The air raids were too frequent and we had already suffered direct hits. Nothing I said had any effect. The girls were too excited at having a chance to be liberated, to be happy and for once feel free! In the end I refused to drink on grounds of my religion, and seeing that I was determined they left me alone, calling me a wet blanket and a fool.

The party livened into an orgy as glass after glass of beer was consumed. The girls collapsed in drunken stupors. Captain Herman was carried to his bunk totally helpless. I assisted some girls to their bunks. Minutes afterwards the air raid sirens sounded, and pandemonium broke loose. The girls screamed, huddled helplessly and terrified on their bunks and in corners. I dragged them out of the hut in case it went on fire. Shrapnel fell around. Bombs whistled down with ear-splitting force and detonated, sending buildings and earth into the air. The sky was lit up by searchlights, gunfire, burning buildings. The camp and factory received direct hits. Next morning as I viewed the smouldering debris I thanked God that once more our work team had been spared. The drinking party was never mentioned.

Relentlessly the bombing continued and eventually we were given orders to abandon the camp!

Each team of girls was ordered to blow up and destroy factory machinery. My task was to pour petrol over the apparatus I had operated and set it on fire. I had no choice. I had to obey. I poured on the petrol and set it alight. Instantly there was an explosion and I was engulfed in flames. Terror stricken and screaming I fled from the building. Seconds later it blew up.

The girls helped to smother the flames. My hair was badly singed; my skin and clothes burned, but I received no medical treatment. Instead I was commanded to assist the other girls set charges which blew up the entire factory. We had to unroll string connected to explosives, light the end and watch the flame travel along. As it reached the detonator we threw ourselves to the floor or ducked for we had not been told how to take safety precautions. When the factory blew up the explosion thundered into the very heavens. The sight was awesome. Flames and sparks leapt hundreds of feet into the sky already blackened with smoke. All this time Allied aircraft dropped bombs, and tracer bullets from German anti-aircraft guns darted overhead. The noise was deafening.

Bewildered, frightened and in great pain I staggered towards the other girls and waited for our orders to join the German army. We were issued with old army overalls or jackets. No helmets or protective clothing of any kind; then assembled to help the troops with food and ammunition.

Prepare To Die!

If we had felt terrorised and desperate before, this new assignment turned us into mechanical subhumans. We lived in a constant state of panic and were brutally ordered to load and unload ammunition, and prepare food for the troops. We retreated from battlefields, ran for cover from air raids and hid during Russian heavy artillery attacks.

In hiding there was a deathly silence. 'Could anyone survive such offensives from the air and land?' I wondered. We crawled for cover in cellars of bombed houses, or hid in bomb craters or holes caused by heavy artillery. The nights were terrifying, the pitch darkness being frequently illuminated by exploding bombs or shell fire. The days were worse. As we became encircled by the Russian battalions and our contingent had neither the resources or the will to fight, survival became the only ultimate aim.

Wherever there was a wood or forest we retreated into it. Emerging we were constantly attacked from the air. Whenever the Russian sorties spotted our convoy they dive-bombed, swooped down firing their guns and encircling us. These manoeuvres were constantly repeated making the German defence useless, for the troops were occupied running to and from their vehicles to escape the onslaught. Whenever there was an opportunity we would clamber back on the trucks and start moving, but as soon as we did the Russian planes were back. I was under orders and would have been shot if seen escaping. On one occasion I stood behind a tree with Russian bullets ricochetting off it, and the ground ploughed up by machine guns. I stared petrified at German lorries loaded with ammunition which were parked only a few yards away and prayed they would not be hit, for I knew we could not survive the explosion.

We endured several days of incessant attacks until the food and ammunition supplies were almost gone. The contingent retreated into the forest. All hope of reaching Berlin and joining the main forces had been abandoned. When darkness fell the soldiers were ordered to line up and stand to attention. The commanding officer looked serious and pale. Addressing his men he said, 'You have fought bravely and honoured the Fatherland. We are now completely encircled by the enemy and outnumbered. We have not enough ammunition to sustain defence for another day and must now consider our position. I do not wish to surrender and so I ask you to prepare to die like heroes.' The soldiers removed their helmets and bowed their heads. I was shocked and bewildered by the ultimatum. The tragic scene moved me deeply and I thought, 'Are they asking God to have mercy on them and their loved ones? All men are alike in the presence of God.' Bowing my head I asked God to forgive them. The private soldiers were so young and like myself were possibly fighting under Hitler's orders and not with their heart or conscience.

I overheard two officers standing near me discussing our fate. 'Shall we shoot the Polaks or leave them to their own fate?' one asked. 'The Russians are heavy vodka drinkers and will do what they like with them. They have no morals and will show no mercy!' It was decided that we should be shot next morning. Everyone was trembling with fear. Occasionally over-tense nerves snapped and deep sobs were heard. I knew I had to escape and made my plans. I asked another girl to join me but she was afraid of being caught.

I was very tired and needed rest, so I crawled away unnoticed to a wooden hut we had used during an attack. No one would risk staying inside it as it stood close to the river within firing range of the Russian attack from the opposite bank. I was too exhausted to care and went inside. After a few hours sleep I crept out under the cover of the bushes and still unobserved made towards the west. It was deathly quiet, no movement or action. From experience I knew that I was in a no man's land with Russians not far away. Tyre marks left by the trucks helped me find my way out of the forest, and I reached the main road by daybreak.

To halt the Allies' advance the Germans had blown up all the bridges and roads not already destroyed by Allied bombing. I crawled on hands and knees; climbed and scrambled over the ruins of bridges. Though filled with foreboding I felt free – free as a bird! I came across the corpse of a German soldier lying on his face. A bullet hole was exactly through the middle of his head. 'The Russian machine-gunners are deadly accurate,' I thought and turned my face away.

All was quiet. No one was about so I ventured on to the road. Turning a sharp corner I stopped dead! I realised with horror that I was walking straight towards the Russian battlefront! Two machine-guns were pointing at me. For a moment I stood paralysed. 'This is the end!' I thought. The Russians didn't shoot. 'Were they under orders not to do so until they had been given the command?' I wondered. Although shaking like a leaf, I pretended not to be afraid and stepping boldly towards them greeted the gunners in Polish. They did not reply or acknowledge that I was there.

I knew I had to be prepared for anything, and once past them quickened my step. Turning a corner I could see in the distance a wooden barrier placed across the road. Beside it were Russian soldiers and a few civilians obviously in a heated dispute. I became afraid and didn't know what to do. Then, as if from nowhere, a man appeared from behind some shrubs and speaking in German whispered, 'Where are you going, child? What are you doing walking alone down this road? All girls are immediately interned by the Russians and the soldiers do what they like with them. Can you see the commotion at the barrier? Get out of here quickly and hide! Go down the hill until you reach a village. It is not yet occupied by the Russians. Hurry you might be in time to hide there! If you see any young women – even foreigners – you may be sure they have been raped and are probably pregnant.' I thanked him and at once left the road and hurried towards the village. Running scared, fear sapping my waning strength, I stumbled over tree roots, slid down wet banks, hid among shrubs, crawled on hands and knees until finally weary and exhausted I reached the village.

The scene was unreal. Women stood about agitated and talking piteously, as if driven out of their minds. There was no other activity; no children about; no men to be seen. The atmosphere was tense. I approached two women. They looked at me astounded.

'Where have you come from?' they asked. The women's voices rose screeching and hysterical with terror. Their eyes were red and anxious.

'Poland!' I replied.

'Get away from here. Quickly!' they shouted. 'The Russians will invade this village any time now. All the young girls are hiding in haystacks or in the woods. Fathers trying to protect their daughters are shot through the head. Some fathers and girls have died already. Get rid of that jacket! It makes it obvious that you worked for the Germans and they will have no mercy on you!'

In spite of their own personal sufferings they showed great kindness and concern for my welfare. From what they knew I deduced that the Russians had been in the area for some time. It was the tactics of the Russians to encircle an area, occupying it and the surrounding villages until they had sufficient reinforcements to advance.

I pleaded with the women to allow me to hide somewhere for I was exhausted and I needed sleep. No one would take responsibility for my safety. Finally one woman pointed to a cellar door at the side of an outside stairway saying, 'A German soldier slept there. You can if you are determined to stay!' With grateful thanks I opened the door and went in. There was some straw on the earthen floor and I sank down on it and soon fell asleep.

Frantic battering on the door woke me up. Women screaming startled me. 'The Russians are here! They stuck their bayonets into everything searching for ammunition and anyone hiding,' they called. 'It is a miracle that they missed the place where you were sleeping. God be praised! But you are still in danger. The soldiers have left for the moment, but they will return. The village is now under Russian occupation.'

Dejected and confused I wandered aimlessly through the streets keeping close to the houses for I dared not be seen. I pleaded for help from the people I met, but was constantly advised to leave.

I was told that at the other end of the village there was a camp abandoned by the German army which had been taken over by refugees and fugitives. It had become a kind of displaced person's refuge. I hurried towards it. All types of people were there – refugees, people deported from their homes by the Nazis into forced labour or prison camps, and homeless German nationals.

There was no-one in charge – no supervision and no discipline. Blankets, clothes and food had been taken from an abandoned Dutch ship moored close by. Everyone helped themselves to what was available. I feared the wild unruly behaviour of the men, but I was now so weak, I decided to stay until I was fit enough to continue my search for my family.

Captive and hunted!
Everything was communal. At night we lay down together, sleeping on straw strewn over the bare floor. The women warned me not to allow myself to be seen during the day. The women in the camp were either engaged, had a partner or were pregnant.

Russian soldiers, usually in pairs, inspected the camp every night. They would enter our sleeping quarters, shine their torches on us and take away any women they wanted. I was warned to hide myself, since most of the women were old or pregnant. I was terrified and prayed hard to be spared. Whenever I had warning of the soldiers' arrival I ran to the back of the camp and into the outside toilet. This 'cat and mouse' predicament continued for some time.

Then one day the patrol came early. It was near mealtime and I was helping the women in the kitchen. I froze! The soldiers entered the kitchen and fondled the women's breasts. I felt sick and wanted to run but knew that any movement could prove my undoing. I slowly and cautiously edged out of the kitchen. Suddenly we were face to face!

'Who are you? Where have you come from? Where are you going?' they asked me with a leering grin.

They addressed me in German but I answered in Polish. 'I am here waiting for my parents. I am from Poland.'

Still talking in German they replied, 'If you are Polish you should go east towards Warsaw. We are going there and will take you with us!'

I persisted replying in Polish saying, 'I want to stay in the camp until my parents are found. After all my home may be destroyed. I know that they will find me here!'

The soldiers would not give in. We argued. They tried to tempt me with sweets. I refused. One said, 'Let's give her vodka. She'll soon be senseless,' and he tried to pour it down my throat. I resisted and struggled with them. They became angry and accused me of being a German spy. I insisted that I was Polish. I knew that if they were convinced that I was a German they could take me and do what they liked with me, but since I was Polish they could be disciplined.

They grew impatient and one of them dragged me

out of the kitchen and behind the camp building. They pushed me against a shed. Physically I was no match for them and I pleaded with them to let me go. As they tore at my clothes I prayed that God would have mercy on me. Suddenly heavy machine gun fire could be heard so loud and incessant one knew it was close by. The soldiers ran to their motorbikes, yelling at me to stay until they returned.

Shaken and weak from the confrontation I dropped to the ground and sobbed desperately. Quite unexpectedly part of the shed tilted open and an old bearded man appeared at the opening.

'What is the matter, child?' he asked.

Like a child clutching her father I clung to him and cried, 'Two Russian soldiers got hold of me and they are coming back. I don't know where to go!'

He looked at me and my torn clothes. I knew he had misunderstood the encounter and thought I had been raped but I had not the strength to explain. Nodding his head sympathetically, he said, 'There is only one place to go child, to the Madonna in the village. She is a very good woman and has helped many a girl in your position. She is the only one who can help you!'

The noise of battle died down – a sign that the Russians had defeated the Germans. They would occupy the area and wait until reinforcements came. Until that time the soldiers could do what they liked. I knew I had to flee!

The old man gave me directions to the Madonna and I hurried away. I found the cottage at the other end of the village, near the bank of the River Havel. I knocked and knocked on the door. A middle-aged woman appeared.

I begged to see the Madonna. In my heart of hearts I did not believe she existed but I was desperate and had no other hope. I was so tired and restless with anxiety. Waiting on the doorstep induced a heavy nauseating sinking sensation. When I felt I could endure it no longer the woman reappeared and I was invited in.

Entering a room I gaped in surprise. Seated in the centre of the room on a high throne-like chair was a frail elderly lady. She was swathed in yards and yards of black silk and lace. Her hair flowed loosely over her shoulders. Her eyes sad, kind, yet determined were fixed on me. They seemed to say, 'I know it all, child, before you speak!'

I stood silent and gazed on her in bewilderment.

She spoke in German, quietly and slowly in a deep voice, 'I know, my child. I have helped many girls like you. Where do you come from?' When I answered, 'Poland', she replied sadly but with a firm finality, 'Yes, there are many like you, but I am sorry I cannot help you. Poor child. Goodbye.'

I was already weak, at the point of collapse, and the shock of the abrupt dismissal left me feeling battered, both mentally and physically. How could anyone who admitted being able to help withhold it from me because I was Polish? A feeling of stubborn pride welled up in me giving me the strength to walk out, dragging my legs as I did so.

Another river to cross!
As I stumbled with bowed head and in tears along the river bank I was reminded of an incident at school involving a bully. He was a plump, physically strong

boy, but below average intelligence.

The school was close to a park, which had a pond we frequented during biology lessons, especially when studying frogs and tadpoles. On an occasion when the teacher was absent the bully caught a cat. He goaded another boy to pull the cat's hindlegs whilst he pulled the forelegs, saying with glee, 'You'll see how funny it is to watch the cat trying to move after her joints are pulled out of place.' I protested strongly and loudly but my pleading fell on deaf ears. The bully jeered at me and called me a soft fool. It was horrible seeing the terrified and tortured animal painfully crawling whilst the boys laughed and chased her. For many years I was haunted by this incident and suffered recurring nightmares. I felt like that cat as I stumbled along the water's edge rejected and in pain.

As I stared into the dark waters desperate thoughts entered my mind, 'I have only to walk in the river and keep walking. There is no-one about. No one to hurt me. What have I to live for anyway? Think of the peace of being still. No more running. No more hunger. No more pain. No more being hunted!' I was taught to believe that suicide is sin, but it did not seem so at this moment – rather a step into peaceful oblivion. I asked myself, 'Does God understand?' I felt certain he did understand my present despair. I looked up into the grey sky and sighed, 'God, please God, let a bullet or a bomb kill me now or I shall drown myself in this river!' It was a frenzied cry from the heart! I waited: nothing happened. Just a still desolate silence.

Slowly my eyes looked down from the sky to the river. Something prompted me to look along the river's edge. At first I doubted what I saw. Not far away was a ship moored on the river bank with a small rowing boat tied to it. The rowing boat bounced up and down merrily, as if inviting me to board it. I hurried towards the ship. There was a light in a cabin and I saw a woman cross the deck and disappear into the turret. I could see she was pregnant. No one else appeared. I hid out of sight but the awful silence and my plight overwhelmed me. I was terrified the Russians would find me. Had they made the old man talk? In my terror I expected the soldiers to appear any moment!

'If only I could cross the river!' I thought wistfully. I looked at the rowing boat bobbing up and down in the swirling waters. It seemed to say, 'Come. I can take you across!' The woman again appeared on the deck.

I rushed towards the ship calling frantically, 'Help me! help me, please!'

She shouted across the waters, 'What is it you want us to do?'

'Hide me till it gets dark. The Russians are after me!' I answered.

Hearing the shouts a man appeared and the woman pleaded with him. 'Hide this poor girl,' she asked.

The ship was Dutch. I presumed that it had got caught in the conflict and held in captivity until the war was over. The man was very reluctant, but the woman, his wife, a kind and compassionate person continued pleading, 'For the sake of our unborn child help this poor girl!'

'There is only the coal hold,' he said relenting, 'and it is full of rats.'

I told him I did not mind. The rats were less a threat

than the Russian soldiers. I realised by now that he was the ship's Captain. He indicated to me to come on board, warning me to keep low and hold firmly on to the wooden ladder stretching from the shore. He insisted that I keep even lower when crossing the deck so as not to be seen, and warned me that the rats would jump on me. I thanked him, climbed into the darkness and he replaced the top.

I was determined not to scream or try to fight off the rats. The pitch darkness of the hold was safer than hiding along the river bank. I stood upright so that the rats could not reach my face. When I was a small child our farm was invaded by rats. They nearly drove Mama out of her mind. At first they were lured to the baits and poison, but soon they became so shrewd nothing could trap them. They never became vicious until pursued or attacked by humans. When Mama was scared by a rat jumping on her dressing table, she panicked and threw her slipper in its direction. The rat leapt at her. She threw herself on to the bed and the rat badly bit her toe. She never threw anything at a rat again.

Several hours passed during which I stood, letting the rats jump over me. I kept my hands hidden and remained as motionless as I could.

Eventually the Captain called me. He opened the hatch, helped me out and bidding me keep low said, 'It is still dark but you cannot stay on the boat throughout the night. The Russians inspect the ship whenever it pleases them, but especially during the early morning. We would all be shot if they find you here. They have already been here half an hour ago. Did you not hear the motorbikes?'

I nodded and said, 'I did hear them and the terror of being discovered made me forget my weariness and fear of the rats.'

I begged him to give me the rowing boat to cross the river, but he shook his head impatiently, saying, 'You do not know what you are suggesting! The Russians are stationed this side of the river with their guns pointing to the other side. The Germans are dug in on the other side with their guns facing this way. In any case there are no boats left. Too many have chosen to escape this way and all the boats are on the opposite shore.'

Desperation made me stand rooted to the deck. 'Getting shot is better than what I am having to endure. I am being hunted like an animal without protection, shelter or food,' I argued.

The woman gave me some porridge in a mess tin, an old dress and a plastic mac as it was now raining and I had no coat. She was kind and concerned and as I left she prayed that God would protect me. I longed to respond by hugging her, but I was too aware of my unclean appearance and could only thank her profusely.

The Captain urged me to follow him, keeping low and close to the bushes where he kept searching for a boat. He tried to make me change my mind, but when I threatened to jump in the river he realised I was serious. He explained that he could not give me his rowing boat as it was his only means of getting to the shore. It was February. The water was icy. The River Havel was wide at this point and known for its dangerous undercurrents and whirlpools. If I was lucky and a boat was found, I would take at least an hour to cross. I felt unwell and knew that the conditions were such that I could easily take cramp. Better to die in the attempt than be captured by the Russians, I decided.

The tireless efforts of the Captain paid off. He found a boat hidden by a covering of thick branches. He untied it, removed the branches, then painstakingly instructed me on how to manoeuvre it. The boat had no oars, but we found a stick nearby, strong enough to help float the boat into the river. There were wooden planks in the boat. The Captain warned me, that I must use them when stepping ashore for there were dangerous bogs which had claimed many victims. He also told me to be as quiet as possible. 'The water carries and resounds noise. Beware of touching or stepping on the chains which are in the boat to secure it to the river bank,' he warned. 'Any noise will alert the armies. Flares will be shot into the sky immediately, and machine guns will aim at any silhouette or shadow in the river.' I thanked him and got into the boat.

The Captain pushed the boat into the river and wished me well. Instantly it spun round and round like a windmill. 'You must be in a whirlpool!' the Captain called, 'That is why the boat is still here. No one was able to get it afloat!' He was soaked to the waist as he stood in the icy waters trying to push me away from the beach. I pushed with the improvised pole and eventually the boat, in a frenzied spin, moved into the river. It was now or never. The boat had to be stopped turning. I dug the pole deep into the riverbed and held on firmly. After several attempts it finally slowed down and flowed with the tide.

Standing upright and with my back to the approaching shore I wiggled the pole and moved across. I thanked God for the dark moonless night and the dank drizzling rain which hid me. In time the shore I had left disappeared from sight.

As I drew closer to the western side of the river the outline of a steep hill became visible against a grey horizon. All was quiet; the only sound the lapping of the ripples I made with the wooden pole. Soon I hit the shore. There were rushes on the river bank, just as the Captain had said. I slid a plank from the boat on to ground and pushed the boat in as far as possible; then silently placing the other plank further on I stepped out of the boat. On hands and knees I crept up the hill under the cover of the long grass. I reached the top unobserved and stood for a moment thanking God. I was comforted by the words from 2 Thessalonians which sprang into my mind – 'The Lord is faithful ... He will strengthen you.'

The Captain had told me that there was a boarding house on the hill which was certain to be filled with fugitives like myself. I might find shelter there. I made towards it. I was wet and cold. The wind began to whistle through the long grass. Dawn was breaking. In my panic I had left the porridge behind in the boat. I was starving and longed to taste it. My teeth were chattering. I was clumsy and shivering when I reached the boarding house. With icy hands I knocked on the main door. No response. I made my way round the house searching and searching for another door. I found one and knocked and knocked until my fists ached. Eventually an angry voice shouted, 'What do you want? Get away! We want some sleep. You are waking up the whole house!'

It was still dark. The rain lashed down and the wind

howled through the trees. My whole body seemed to turn to ice and my heart suddenly began to pound. I was frantic and continued to bang on the door until at last a light came on. I was standing on a veranda looking into a room filled with beds. Angry faces peered from the duvets. The beds were all occupied but the sight of such comfort filled me with an uncontrollable longing. I shouted, 'I will not stop knocking until you give me shelter!'

With shouts of swearing and cursing the door opened and an old man told me to be quiet and not disturb his guests. Then seeing me he immediately took pity on me and said, 'Follow me. The house is full up with guests and such as yourself. I could be in serious trouble for sheltering you. All I have left is a barn attic which is full up, too, but there is straw on the floor and you will be out of the rain.' Warning me to crouch low and keep close to the wall so as not be seen, he took me to the barn. Placing a ladder against the wall he knocked on a small wooden hatch under the barn roof. 'Open up!' he shouted, 'I have a young girl. Move over and let her in!' There was the sound of disgruntled voices and shuffling, then the hatch opened and I climbed in onto a bare floor. The roof was low, too low to stand up. I crawled over legs and boots and huddled down. The opening closed. It was pitch black.

The silence was interrupted by snoring and coughing – incessant coughing. I sensed that the occupants were men, but what did I care? What did anyone care? We might be inanimate discarded objects without feelings. Better out of sight, out of mind! I started shivering and could not stop. The floorboards seemed to be shaking with me. A man's voice called out, 'Here girl! You can't sit up all night. Here is some straw. Lie down on it.' Pushing his neighbour's legs he pulled a little straw from under himself. I took it, thanked him and crouched down.

As I lay in the dark I listened to the wind whistling against the roof. It reminded me of our barn in Poland and the times we played among the sweet smelling hay and straw. Would I ever see my home again? Suddenly I longed for nothing else than a bath, or just a wash – some warm water and a towel – and home! As I fell into a disturbed sleep my thoughts were on home and my family.

We were awakened by banging on the hatch and a man's voice calling. I expected the hatch to open and another fugitive clamber in. The voice was that of the old man. He was clearly agitated and ordered all of us: 'Get out and away! You can't stay here. Now be on your way before you are caught!' One by one we hurried out into the cold, the rain and the darkness.

I was desperate to have a wash, so I waited until the others had slipped away. Approaching the man I said, 'Sir, I am sorry for disturbing you last night. You have been very kind. Thank you.'

He looked at me quizzically, and with a mischievous grin replied, 'Don't mention it, girl!' He beckoned me, 'Come round here and keep quiet! I am the manager of this guesthouse and serve lunch to my guests. Keep out of sight but come to the dining room at quarter past eleven.' He pointed to a door, 'That's the main door to the dining hall over there. I'll give you something to eat.'

'But-t-t,' I stammered, 'I haven't any money!'

'That's alright. Worry about it when you have eaten,' he replied, smiling.

Encouraged by his goodwill, I asked, 'Sir! There is one thing I wish more than anything else!'

'And what would that be?' he enquired.

'Some warm water, a towel and privacy to wash myself!' I begged.

'Alright! You can go into the back kitchen,' he replied.

It was a simple small stone-floored room with a peat fire over which hung a copper pot filled with steaming hot water. A towel and a small piece of soap lay close by. How precious the water and the soap were! If I had been given all the perfumes of Arabia they could not have cleansed or refreshed me as the warm soapy lather did. I washed and washed myself, wallowing in the experience. I swilled my underwear, singeing them in my haste to get them dry enough to wear again.

If I had any suspicions regarding the old man's integrity my gnawing hunger drove them away. I waited longingly for the appointed time to arrive and kept glancing through the kitchen window where I could see the clock. The place was quiet and deserted. I wondered when the guests would arrive. At quarter past eleven I opened the heavy wooden door leading to the dining hall and stood puzzled. The room was empty. Not wanting to be conspicuous I chose a table in the darkest corner anticipating that guests would arrive and occupy the others. No one came.

After I had been sitting for some time the manager came through the door carrying a tray. He bowed and greeted me with, 'Good day!' then walked out. He returned bringing cutlery which he placed on my table and then left again. I waited. The anticipation of a meal made me desperately hungry. The manager reappeared with a bowl of steaming hot soup, a piece of bread and salt and pepper. It was all so unreal after my past experiences. The room was dark with shuttered windows and a heavy door which remained closed. It had a cocktail bar which obviously had been out of use for a long time.

'Where are the other guests?' I wondered. 'Had I been duped?' Shrugging off my suspicions I thought, 'What does it matter? I am starving and cold. The hot soup was most welcoming no matter how it tasted!' I added seasoning and relished the few pieces of carrots and potatoes floating in the watery liquid.

The manager returned smiling and asked, 'Is it good?'

'Yes. Very good.' I replied gratefully. 'Thank you so very much!'

He removed the bowl and spoon and returned with a little mashed potato and cabbage. My hopes began to rise and I expected a sweet and a drink, for I was still very hungry and undernourished. It seemed so ungrateful to be disappointed when the man took the plate away and said, 'That is it, dear!'

I made to leave, thanking him and apologising for not being able to pay but he stopped me, saying, 'Forget it!' and came uncomfortably close. I again thanked him and hurried away. As I was closing the door he called, 'Come again tomorrow at the same time!'

It was my intention to move on, but I was still very weak; therefore I joined some of the men who had slept in the loft who were hiding in the shadow of the building. In whispers we enquired about each other – 'Where were we going? Where had we come from?'

It was late in the afternoon when one of the men asked me, 'Have you got anything to eat?' I shook my head and without anyone seeing him he took a piece of bread from his pocket and gave it to me saying, 'Put it away out of sight of the others!' Hiding the morsel of bread behind my back I slunk round the corner and ate it hungrily. I felt I could trust this man and confided in him that it was my plan to move on.

He advised me against it, saying, 'That would be very foolish. You look ill and are obviously very weak. Without food or shelter you may not survive. At least here you have a roof over your head and something to eat once a day. The Russians are now very close and there is no knowing what could happen to you travelling alone in open country.'

I was indeed weak and agreed to stay. They were decent men who treated me with respect; fugitives, like myself, and too concerned about their existence and forebodings. I was glad, when lying shivering with cold in the loft, to have the warmth of another human close to me, and grateful when someone reached over to give me a corner of their blanket. We left the loft early each morning, making sure that if the loft was searched in our absence there was no evidence of anyone having slept there. Always on the alert we stayed huddled together in the shadow of the guesthouse.

The days passed and I continued to go for my midday meal. It became obvious that the old man hoped for some reward, perhaps only a kiss or two. At the same time he did not want to frighten me away or appear bold. I had resolved when very young that I would not kiss a man until I was engaged, and although I pitied the old man I knew I could not allow him to take liberties with me. I therefore made up my mind to leave without telling anyone, for I did not want to be dissuaded. Asking God to be gracious to the old man I prepared to leave.

It was still dark when we left the loft and so I joined the men in the shadows. The past days had been uncomfortably quiet. The men were of the opinion that the Russians on the other side of the River Havel still believed that the Germans were dug in on this side ready to defend any offensives.

I told them about my escape; that I had crossed the river in a rowing boat. They were surprised and one said, 'You were lucky, for at six o'clock that night the Germans threw their guns and rifles into the river and fled!'

'Lucky indeed,' I thought. 'But more than that, it was further proof of God's protection and love, for had I been a few hours earlier I may not have survived.' I looked at the young men and wondered if they were German deserters disguised as civilians.

Someone shouted, 'There they are! They are coming!'

'Who?' we all asked. 'Where?'

We edged our way along the wall staring in the direction of a pointing finger. Indeed *they* were coming! It was like watching a film. Moving over the horizon a convoy of tanks, horse-drawn gun-carriages and infantry advanced unhindered.

'It's the Russian reinforcements!' someone shouted.

'So that's what they have been waiting for!'

It was indeed the Russian army advancing to occupy this part of Germany without any opposition. Even at a distance we could recognise the soldiers. Their overcoats had a distinctive way of swaying in the wind. The infantry guided horses which were hunched under the weight of heavy loads. Soon the convoy was nearing the guesthouse and the danger of being encircled was imminent.

I did not wait to observe the advancing Russians for long. Even though the invasion was anticipated, fear gripped my heart. I felt sick and turned pale.

One of the men asked anxiously, 'Are you afraid?'

I replied, 'Oh yes! I must go! Which is the best way to try and escape the invading army?'

He tried to reassure me, 'There will be others running to escape when they see this, for there is sure to be fighting. The way to the village is best.'

I was terrified and, bidding my companions goodbye, I ran!

It was slow progress walking through the woods and I feared that the contingent would soon overtake me. Any minute I expected a Russian soldier to jump out from behind a tree. Pulling my scarf around my face I walked with bent head and pretended to be an expectant mother. Reaching the village I tried to find someone who could direct me towards the west. I knocked on the doors of several houses before getting a reply. The occupants were startled at my news. They panicked shouting, 'Oh God, what shall we do? Where shall we go?' and without stopping to answer me they ran off to alert their neighbours.

Eventually I saw a young man and woman loading bundles and clothing on bikes. I ran to them. They told me that they were fleeing to escape the Russians. 'We have friends who will give us shelter for the night if we are lucky enough to reach them,' the young man told me. 'You can join us if you wish.' I accepted the offer eagerly.

Another journey as a fugitive began. Were they husband and wife, or brother and sister, I wondered? Married or unmarried it mattered little. We were human beings with the same fear and in the same struggle to survive: young people ready to abandon our homes for a faith, a principle and often placing ourselves in greater danger.

It was to prove a long and arduous trek. With no time to stop, eat or rest we hurried on. I had travelled mostly on foot halfway across Poland and Germany, although I had taken time to rest. I had great admiration for my companions. They were tired and driven by fear too, with the same determination to survive.

The hours passed and it seemed that we would never arrive at our destination that night. My whole body ached with every movement. Pains shot up my legs. I was thirsty and hungry, and was grateful when the young woman gave me an apple and a piece of bread to eat as we walked on. Fortunately the land was flat. My companions pushed their bikes.

When walking through a wood I begged to sit down for a while, but the man said, 'It is unwise. If you are as tired as that and give in to sit down, you will never be able to get up again.' I realised that they had rested and eaten well before leaving. They were leaning on the bikes for support as they walked. I asked if I could be allowed to push one. The woman agreed and it did help me. The country track had furrows like some country lanes in Poland. I led the bike along the furrows so that I could ease my weight on to it.

We arrived after midnight at the home of my companions' friends. Our unexpected arrival caused some disquiet and confusion. Our welcome was lukewarm. 'Were they just afraid?' I wondered. I was conscious of repeatedly being scrutinised, but was too tired to care. I just wanted to lie down somewhere and sleep. Whilst we drank black coffee our situation was discussed and plans made.

The hosts were afraid to give us shelter. They said that if the Russians discovered that they were harbouring escapees everyone would be shot. Obviously it was more dangerous to be found running away from the Russians than staying at home pretending to welcome them. They gave us permission to sleep in their barn, but we had to promise, in the event of being discovered, to say that they did not know we were there. We had to creep in without being seen, and leave before dawn unnoticed. As an added precaution we could not be provided with blankets.

We crept in the barn and dug ourselves into the straw. I shivered from the extreme cold, but finally fell asleep from sheer exhaustion. We were awakened by our hosts nervously calling, as if under their breath, 'Get up! Get up! and move on before daybreak.'

It was dark and cold as we made our way across open country. I thanked God for leading me to my companions, Stan and Marlene, for I would never have found my way through the many winding lanes nor over the rivers. Stan knew the land well. When we came to a bridge we had to cross, it was destroyed by the retreating German army. Stan urged us on saying, 'Hurry! If the next bridge across the river is blown up before we reach it, we will be in trouble as there are no boats left on this side, and the river is too dangerous and wide to swim across unaided! It is too much to hope that the ferry is still in use!'

We hurried on and on. It was now a matter of life or death. The next bridge was also blown up, but Stan was still resourceful. He knew where a friend had hidden a boat. He had certainly laid careful plans for his escape!

The boat was found hidden in bushes. It was, however, too small to take us, bikes and all, in one crossing. I thought I would be left behind, but they intended that I should go with them, and after two very precarious crossings we made it. Stan hid the boat before we continued on our journey. We arrived late at night at a farm. Only as I entered the farmyard did I realise how hungry and tired I was. Fear had driven us on regardless of our weakness without eating or resting.

The farmer and his wife welcomed us. We were offered a supper of jacket potatoes which was all the food they had. It had been months since they had eaten anything else. Eagerly we watched our hostess tip a large pot of steaming hot potatoes onto the wooden table. We said grace and ate the potatoes with our fingers. It was too dangerous to leave evidence that anyone had been given hospitality and it was for that reason we were not given plates or cutlery. The farmer was restless and uneasy until we had eaten and the table wiped clean. It was wonderful for me to sit and eat until my hunger was satisfied and I said so and expressed my gratitude.

The situation was too grave for casual talk and only plans for our escape were discussed. It was agreed that we must all be ready to leave at a moment's notice. Stan, Marlene and myself were to sleep in the barn.

God was good to me. I was grateful for my companions' help and trust, for I would not have been so fortunate without them. The farmer and his wife often looked at me with deep concern and I felt that they were anxious about my fate, travelling alone in such violent times. But I was now feeling more confident. I had a pact with God. He wanted me for full-time service and I had prayed to him to keep my soul and body whole, or not at all! I surged with new hope, new courage. I would be spared and greater determination to survive assailed me.

It was still dark when we left next morning. The farmer had warned Stan that both the bridge and ferry were out of action, but that a German officer and some of his men were transporting troops across by boat. The officer was kind and sympathetic and had allowed civilians to cross as well. We might be lucky.

There was an endless queue when we arrived at the river bank. The German officer looked tired and frustrated. People were begging to be ferried across and he was unable to refuse. We pleaded with him, but when he saw the bicycles he said, 'No! It is not possible to put bikes and luggage in the boat when so many people need to be rescued. It is out of the question. I am sorry!' Most people had some luggage. I was the only one with absolutely nothing – only what I wore.

After we had waited on the shore for some hours I could see that time was running out for us. I turned to Stan and Marlene and said, 'I don't want to leave you for I could not have come this far without your help, but it may be that we won't get across together. I would like to try once more.' They both agreed that I should try alone and wished me well. I thanked my companions, arranging to wait for them at the other side and approached the officer, 'Please let me on! There is room for just one more and as you see I have no baggage!' He nodded his approval.

The boat was seriously overloaded and a keen wind whipped up the waves, but after a perilous crossing we landed. I stood on the shore confused and lost. 'What should I do now?' I wondered. I waited for some hours. My companions did not come, and at last after seeking directions to Westerstede I set off alone.

Where to go?
So much was happening that the sequence of events is now blurred and confused. I often walked alone through woods, sleeping under bushes or barns. Occasionally I met up with other refugees and accompanied them. Sometimes I joined groups making their escape to the west. It was a race on foot away from the advancing Russians. It was a cruel time, especially for girls, mothers and babies.

A young woman, thin and exhausted, pleaded with a driver for a lift on his laden cart. The man was sorry but he could not risk the extra weight. She kept pleading with him and in the end he agreed to carry her suitcase. Some hours later the woman could not be seen. It was impossible to look for her among the crowds of refugees. The driver opened the case hoping that there would be some identification. We were horrified! In the case was a baby, well wrapped but stiff and dead! Did the mother hope that the suitcase would be opened in time to save her child, I wondered? If she knew it was dead surely she would have buried it rather than carry the heavy load? Who were we to judge such actions when our world had come to an end and all we faced was a dark abyss?

I travelled mostly by night, and when possible through woods and forests. I relied, like a hunted animal, on a sixth, or was it a seventh, sense? I developed an instinct for signs which alerted me to the presence of the Russian army in the area. Seeing tank tracks I crawled so as not to be seen and shot at. I threw myself on to the ground, in a ditch – anywhere – at the sight of anything moving. Several times when I saw the shadowy outline of an armed soldier I lay still for hours.

I was alone and approaching the brow of a hill when I found myself face to face with a Russian tank, guns at the ready. I dared not retreat as this would arouse suspicion. I broke out in a cold sweat as the likelihood of being shot at became apparent. I had no choice but to put on a brave face and walk straight on. I felt doomed, as if walking to my execution, like the time when I faced the Russian machine-gunners. I didn't see or hear anyone and walked on. It was typical of Russian soldiers to sit motionless without turning their heads unless their suspicions were aroused. I continued until it was too dark to go on and lay among some shrubs lonely and afraid of being discovered!

Eventually I reached a village east of the River Elbe. In contrast to the many deserted places I had left, this village was teeming with people – a motley crowd of refugees trapped in a dead end. The German army was dug in on the east side of the Elbe and the American army along the banks of the west side. Behind us the Russians were advancing.

There were long lines of people. I was curious and as I went towards one I overheard the word 'Bread'. I ran! The expectation of something to eat aroused a desperate gnawing hunger. There were two queues. One where you obtained a bread coupon, a small scrap of paper on which you wrote your name, and the other where you were handed a bread roll. My hunger became primitive, animal like. I had to have bread! I grew impatient and agitated. The supply was limited and I feared there would be none left when it came my turn. The rolls were small and oval, similar to a continental roll. They were cut in half and on producing my ticket I was given one half.

I was starving, the smell of the bread aroused my taste buds and increased the pangs of hunger, but I resisted eating it all at once. I knew what it was like to be on the point of starvation and have no food. I sat down away from the crowds and drew imaginary lines across the half roll just as I had done in the labour camp. One piece for each day. I savoured a portion, hardly a mouthful, and hid the rest.

Because the village was so overcrowded with homeless people there was no hope of finding shelter. I decided to move on and get as near the River Elbe as was possible. The path from the village broke up into several winding footpaths. The land was boggy with treacherous sinking sands. Occasionally there were clumps of small shrubs where the soil was drier. Looking around I realised that one could get lost very easily. It was like a labyrinth of narrow paths and reminded me of a board game we played as children 'How to find your way home?'

I was contemplating the most direct and safest route to the river when I saw a cyclist skilfully making his way along one of the paths. As he came closer I noticed he was wearing a German uniform. He stopped and asked where I was going. I begged him to show me the way to the river. I followed him for some time and he assured me that there was a farm nearby where I could find shelter. He warned me that unless we travelled quicker we could be stranded among the bogs in the dark and he offered me a lift sitting on the bar of his bike. It was the most uncomfortable and precarious ride. There were ponds on both sides of the narrow path and I knew that my slightest movement could overbalance the bike throwing us into the water. We travelled in silence, concentrating on the hazards ahead until we were in sight of a lonely farmstead.

As we approached the soldier mumbled, 'I must report you to my superior officer. I am only a sergeant, but I will personally be responsible for your safety!' The news stunned me! I was shaken and frightened. That I was being led into a trap and captivity never entered my head.

I was escorted to the guard room. The sergeant

clicked his heels, saluted his officer and gave an account of our meeting. The officer dismissed him. I grew alarmed! The sergeant was clearly upset and enquired as to what would become of me. The officer replied, 'This is my business. The girl is now my internee!' The sergeant became angry and insisted, 'I brought her and am responsible for her well-being. I have given her my word, and will make sure she is unharmed!' Tempers flared. At that moment I could not see the sense of the outrage. Only afterwards did I realise the seriousness of my position.

The sergeant was clearly a man of moral courage. He refused to give in, and finally it was agreed that I would remain unmolested and sleep with another girl in an upstairs room. The sergeant took me to the room and said, 'You can wash and then have supper downstairs.'

The room was comfortably furnished and clean. I could not believe my eyes. There was a bed with a clean duvet and pillows, such as we had in Poland. It was such a long time since I had looked at myself in a mirror and I was distressed at what I saw. I looked awful – dirty and in rags. My hair was filthy and matted. My usually fair skin mud-spattered, weather beaten and raw. I washed my body and my hair. Borrowing a brush and comb from the dressing table I groomed my long flaxen hair. It was wonderful, unbelievable. Yet, a fear gnawed in my mind. The girl, Greta, with whom I shared the room, came in and we soon became friends. She had no objections to sharing the bed with me.

We were called to supper. The officers, the sergeant, the farmer and his family sat round a large table which was covered with a clean cloth and set with cutlery. The farmer's wife placed a large bowl of steaming hot jacket potatoes in the middle of the table. Beside it was a bowl of gravy and a ladle. It was a delicious meal. Encouraged by the sergeant I ate until I was completely satisfied.

After supper everyone sat around relaxed, laughing and chatting. I was very tired and thanking the farmer's wife I withdrew to my room and slept soundly.

After my past experiences this seemed too good to be true. Next day, I tried to befriend the farmer's wife, thanking her and offering to help in anyway, even milking the cows. She was surprised and replied, 'There is not much to do but if you wish you can help with the milking any time!'

The officer asked to see me. He had piercing blue eyes and I felt uncomfortable in his presence. He approached me saying, 'You are my internee and I am at liberty to do with you anything I want!' He grabbed me round the waist and drew me to him. I winced and called out, 'Please, let me go!' The farmer's wife came into the room and he released me. I tried from now on to keep out of his way. I knew I must leave soon – but how could I get away and where would I go?

Next day the officer again called me to his room. He was more composed and told me that he had plans to escape with his men before the Russians came. They preferred to be captured by the Americans. He pointed to a map, saying, 'Here is a dry dock. There is a boat in which we can make our escape. The water can be raised allowing it to float into the river and across the Elbe!' I was suspicious wondering why he was confiding in me, but I said nothing.

During the daytime Greta avoided me and was not seen around the farm. I wondered where she went. One evening she invited me to accompany her. I had no reason to refuse and went with her. We walked along a field to an underground shelter. She called out and the ground opened revealing an entrance and a ladder. She descended and asked me to follow. I was fascinated and curious. I never imagined such places existed. It was like a mine and very low. We had to bend or sit. I soon realised that it was an army defence – a dugout.

Greta introduced me to the soldiers who were unoccupied and lazing about. I responded in a ladylike manner, hoping for some interesting conversation after my long days of solitude. I plied the soldiers with questions, 'Where are you from? What do you feel about the whole business of war? Do you know where your families are?' The soldiers stared at me.

Getting no response, a very uncomfortable feeling swept over me. Then the whole bizarre situation began to dawn on me. How naive I was! I sat bolt upright and became silent. Mixed-up feelings such as I had never experienced before welled inside me. There was a barrier around me and no communication could be established. I felt it was not my fault, yet I felt guilty for being there.

An elderly soldier shouted out in a chiding voice, 'Take that girl out of here at once. She is an innocent girl!' Greta looked frightened, scrambled to her feet and led me out.

That night I talked seriously with Greta. She had become more open since the incident in the dugout and confessed that she was a married woman. I had not the heart to condemn her. Brought up in a sheltered Christian home, and living protected in the country, what did I know how others lived, felt and thought.

I asked her, 'Surely you love your husband! Don't you feel remorse when giving yourself to any man who wants you?'

To my astonishment she replied, 'No! The world is sad enough. One might as well get from life what little pleasure you can. The same applies to the soldiers.'

I asked, 'What would you think if your husband knew? How might he react?'

'I might never see him again anyway,' she replied. 'We might both be dead soon. What does it matter. I hope he is having pleasure in the same way!'

'And what if you both are spared and reunited,' I persisted, 'How would you both feel then?'

Greta looked surprised and unsure of herself. Without answering me she promised to try and escape with me next day. We both agreed that it was not good for us to remain any longer.

I confided in the farmer's wife. I knew I had no chance of escaping unless I had an alibi. Greta could come and go as she pleased, for everyone knew where she was going and would have little difficulty getting away. The farmer's wife agreed to wake me at 5 am to help her with the milking. She told me that some miles along the river there was a neutral zone where the Americans were helping refugees to cross. This was the information I wanted, an answer to prayer. Spurred on by this new hope we made our plans.

At 5 am the farmer's wife called us. I dressed quickly, putting on the dress and plastic mac the ship captain's wife had given me. Making sure I still had the piece of bread I left with Greta.

'Where are you going?' shouted the sentry as we approached. Greta had no problem. She was allowed to pass.

'I am going to help the farmer's wife with the milking,' I replied, and held up the bucket.

The farmer's wife stood close by and said, 'Yes. The girl has kindly offered to help me and I am grateful.'

The sentry looked at my mac and I quickly explained, 'I am cold and am wearing this mac as it is the only coat I have.' He grinned mischievously and beckoned me to pass.

I helped with the milking. The farmer's wife spoke very little, perhaps because she had seen so much. When I suggested that I should now try to leave the barn before she did, she agreed. There was no-one about and I hurried out and into the fields. Greta was waiting for me and we immediately hurried north along the river bank of the Elbe.

All too soon Greta became very tired. She was in a poor physical condition and, unlike me, had not walked for a long time. We rested frequently, but it was obvious that she could not continue. She became anxious about holding me back. In the end she decided that she had no alternative but to go back to the farm. She did have food and shelter there and the soldiers would soon be leaving. I was sorry to see her go. She had made a positive effort to leave, but her health had let her down. Feeling sad and lonely I stood watching Greta disappear from view.

There was no time, however, to stand and wallow in self-pity. I walked on and on along the embankment. I grew disappointed and disheartened for there was no activity on the river bank. Agonising doubts about the existence of a neutral zone flooded my mind. It was very cold. The sun, although shining and sparkling on the waters, did nothing to warm the air. My body was weary. I decided to rest and eat a crumb of the bread roll. I drank from the river and ate the bread but this did nothing to revive me. The urgency of finding the crossing made me restless, and although exhausted I continued my journey.

After some time I spotted in the distance an open beach. There was a ship crossing to the other side. I became excited. The beach seemed peppered with black spots, some larger than others. 'Were they people?' I wondered, and hurried on. Soon I began to recognise people huddled on the open grassy bank. Some had improvised tents, and there were a number of horse-drawn carts. I rushed towards the crowds.

If I expected a welcoming response when I arrived, I was bitterly disappointed. I felt lonelier than ever in this diverse crowd. I tried to make my way through but was shouted at, 'Stay at the side. We are all queuing and have been for days. Everyone has to take their proper turn ...' I could do nothing but squat on the ground at the edge of the crowds and study the people. There were many families of all nationalities. There were some German soldiers; some with motorbikes and all with rifles.

I watched the ship cross from the other side. It was late afternoon when it eventually berthed. Orders were shouted from the ship and people began to board. The German soldiers were searched and after they had thrown their rifles into the river were allowed on board. The entire operation was conducted on a makeshift wooden bridge. The Americans never left the ship. When it was fully loaded it sailed away.

Dusk fell but the ship did not return. When it was dark a woman and two men beckoned me. They had seen me arrive; watched whilst I sat alone and took pity on me. I was invited to share a tin of sardines with them and encouraged to drink some oil. Normally I would have baulked at the very thought, but I took some. I was not nauseated and the oil made me feel better.

Feeling guilty about my piece of bread, I produced it and asked them to share it, but one of the men said, 'Keep it as it is all the food you have. Now let's hurry. We must find shelter or we will perish from the cold. We know of an army dugout and might be able to sneak in, especially if the soldiers are on duty all night.' Keeping low and silent we reached the dugout and crawled in one by one. There was some straw and soon we were feeling cosy and warm. I was just dropping off to sleep when a light shone from the opening and an angry voice ordered us out.

It was now very dark and we could see only faint shadows. We squeezed out of the dugout as fast as we could into a downpour of rain. One of the men said, 'I know where we can find shelter under a tin roof. A farmer keeps the straw for his cattle in it. We must hurry or all the space will be taken.' It was so dark we followed in a line. We crossed a ploughed field. The furrows were filled with water and we sank or became stuck in the soft wet earth. Unable to pierce the darkness we trod all over the place until we were sodden and cold.

The man whispered, 'Here it is!' We looked. A black shadow was looming before us. It was the shelter, four pillars supporting a tin roof. We were exposed to the wind and rain, so we tried to arrange the bales of straw so that we could sleep on them or lie against them. I found it impossible. The bales were too heavy and large, and would not separate. It was very cold. The wind and rain lashed our bodies and we were glad to have the warmth of another body close to us. I had only a fitful sleep; partly because of the old men snoring and partly because my feet were wet and cold. Travelling alone and being so young I realised more and more how vulnerable I was and how much I depended on God's mercy and protection.

As soon as it was daylight we returned to the queue. My companions had several tins of sardines and I was given a share each time they ate. The thundering roar of gunfire grew louder as the Russians advanced. The first ship berthed in the late afternoon, filled up, left and returned but still we were a long way behind in the queue.

The sun setting in the west paled into insignificance as the eastern sky emblazed with the fires of the Russian advance. There was a hush among the waiting crowd. If the boat did not return and we were stranded another night on the shore, what would the morning bring?

5

Gone to Earth
February-May, 1945

So many rivers to cross

The sky in the east was awesome darkened by dense smoke and alight with leaping flames as the Russians advanced. If the reality of the scene had not been so terrifying and tragic the spectacle would have bordered on the theatrical, for the show of force was never resisted. The Russians seemed intent on displaying their might by destroying and killing anything which crossed their path.

The thunder of artillery fire was ear-splitting as the army drew nearer. I stood petrified as the possibility of being left on the shore slowly became a reality, for I knew that anyone fleeing from the Russians was considered by them a deserter from Communism and punished without mercy.

We watched the ship sail across the Elbe to the American zone, and waited anxiously for it to return. Surely it must come! Then, like the messenger of doom, a voice through a loud speaker, boomed from the opposite side of the river, 'Everyone leave the shore at once! The Russians are arriving soon. The Americans and Russians are allies and you must now seek their protection! Move!'

There was a sudden hush. The crowd just sat as if turned to stone, unable to take in the significance of the order. The voice grew impatient and shouted, 'Leave the shore at once or we will shoot!' The people jumped to their feet in a mad scramble and shrieking with terror ran for their lives.

I was too stunned to move. I could not believe that having endured so much, travelled so far my hopes of reaching my family would end like this! I watched the frenzied flight of human wretches, then turned to stare at the forbidden shore as if nailed to the ground.

Suddenly two bullets whistled past my ear. A young boy shouted, 'Get down or you'll be shot!'

It was obvious the Americans were in earnest. Were they, I wondered, anxious not to offend the Russians by continuing to rescue refugees who were fleeing from them? Where would I go? Where would I seek refuge when the Americans were now abandoning us? Two more bullets whistled past bringing me to my senses. I threw myself flat on the ground beside the young boy. He whispered, 'We will have to lie still until it gets dark.'

Only when we could no longer see the other shore did we move. Cautiously we rose to our feet and looked at each other. The boy was small and frail.

'Where are you going? How old are you?' I asked.

Stephen replied, 'I am thirteen. I want to reach my Grannie's home and need to cross the Elbe. Weren't you afraid when the Americans threatened to shoot and the bullets whizzed past you?"

I was won over by the boy's spirit and determined attitude. He inspired me not to give in. I had already come this far in spite of the hardships and setbacks, and with God's grace would win through. There was an instinctive bonding between us like brother and sister. He could have been Felix, I thought. I would stay with him and surely in the end we would each reach our destination.

Darkness was falling and we had to find shelter, or perhaps a boat. It was more than likely that all the boats had been confiscated and were now moored on the other side, but as my past experiences had proved, there was always a chance of finding one. Seeking the protection of the shrubs we crept towards the river's edge, and groping in the dark searched every bush. After some time we stumbled upon a large hole.

'There will be room for us in here and we can shelter from the wind and cold until daybreak,' I whispered.

A voice coming from inside the cave threatened us, 'Get out of here! Who are you anyway?'

Startled, I stammered, 'We are just looking for a boat to cross the river!'

A ragged young man, frightened and pale appeared. Seeing us he relaxed and taking pity on us he said, 'Come in. There is room for you.'

The man with no name
We could tell by the man's awkward movement that he was disabled. 'Was he a German deserter?' I wondered. He was obviously shaken at being discovered and was wary of us. He told us that he also wanted to cross the Elbe. Possibly because he could not do so by himself his attitude softened and he confided in us that he knew where a boat was hidden. There were, however, no oars.

He asked if we would go out and look for anything which could be used, preferably planks of wood.

I ventured out, Stephen following me. It was very dark except for the searchlight positioned in the American zone. Groping and feeling the ground with our hands we searched. I stretched out at what appeared to be black marks on the beach and touched strips of old boards. I winced as my hand was pierced by some nails. We were elated at our find and carried the wood back in high spirits.

We did not know the name of the young man and decided to call him 'Noname'.

Noname eagerly grabbed the planks, and without wasting any time, he handed one to Stephen and ordered us to follow quietly and cautiously. The searchlights continued to scan the shore and we had frequently to throw ourselves on the ground and lie still. The man led the way. He looked into the bushes, glanced round from time to time, and kept beckoning us to keep within the cover of the bushes away from the beam of the searchlight. Eventually, we reached a cove-like inlet. Noname hurried us on. The boat was still there and we ran towards it. I thought it odd that it was not secured in any way. As we clambered in our companion warned us, 'Whatever you do, avoid touching the chains which are in the bottom of the boat. Any noise could betray us.'

We felt pleased with ourselves and happy at what we had achieved so far. Stephen and I were handed the makeshift oars, whilst Noname pushed the boat off the sand and hopped in urging us to row hard. As soon as we did so the boat went into a wild spin and turned back into the cove to the spot where we found it. We continued to try to row out in this way but it was of no avail. We became exhausted. Noname was up to his knees in the cold waters. In the end we all sank despairingly into the boat as it dawned on us why it was still there!

The swirling waters of the cove formed into a whirlpool causing the boat to spin round until it became stuck in the sand. 'Why was it there?' I wondered. 'Had someone been shot trying to cross, and the oars accidentally let fall into the river?' I shuddered at the possibilities. Gazing despondently into the waters my attention was drawn to a piece of wood spinning madly just as the boat had done. Suddenly it occurred to me that a whirlpool must inevitably have a central point of pressure where the waters are forced to change direction and move against the tide. If we could reach this point we might get sufficient force to enable us to get clear and out of the cove into the river. I became animated and explained my theory to my companions.

They looked dubious at first and then agreed to try. We pushed the boat along the side of the cove letting it gather momentum, and then rowed hard into the current, instead of away from the shore as we had been doing. The boat lurched dangerously and it took our combined efforts to manoeuvre it out and away from the jutting headland. Exerting all our strength we rowed hard, Noname and Stephen with the oars and I with the wood I found in the cove. Suddenly the boat moved into the swirling waters of the river and the force of the current swept it away. Tossing and turning violently the boat spun round and round. Noname called out, 'Hold it! Hold it!' We gripped the oars tightly trying to stop the boat from spinning, and not until we were well into the flow of the river was it controlled.

In our confusion we had failed to see protruding rocks and small islets ahead of us. They loomed up dangerously as the boat sailed towards them. At the same time we were caught in the full beam of a search-light and our outline was reflected in the waters.

Noname called desperately, 'Get down! Get down! and row for all your worth. Our lives depend on it! We are in danger of being grounded on the rocks or an islet or being shot at!' In an alarmed voice he asked, 'Which side did we leave? What directions should we take?' We were panic-stricken! No one knew!

We fell into a numbed silence, and let the boat drift on. I prayed and concentrated hard. A picture of the wood I had seen spinning in the cove sprang into my mind. I had spotted the wood by the light of the search-light coming from the left. I shouted in excitement, 'The searchlight was on our left when we started from the cove!' On our way, creeping low behind bushes and concentrating on getting away, we had forgotten to take account of our position. We had not reckoned on being spun around until we had lost all sense of direction. What seemed so simple, getting from A to B, nearly proved a fatal disaster. The searchlight intended for our destruction had proved, instead, to be our salvation.

Recovering our composure we concentrated on get-ting across without being seen and shot at. We were a bizarre crew! Noname and Stephen rowed hard with wooden planks and I sat at the back manoeuvring the stick in the way the Dutch Captain had taught me.

We eventually landed in a small cove protected by an overhanging cliff edge. Noname urged us on, saying, 'It is a matter of life or death. Quick! On to the grass and off the beach. We must get out of the range of the searchlight before anyone hears or sees us!' Pulling ourselves up by the branches of an overhanging tree we ran from the shore. Suddenly shots were fired. 'They are lighting up the entire countryside! They have heard us,' whispered Noname. 'Lie low; faces down; hands hidden and don't move until I tell you!' The night turned into daylight and seemed to remain like that for an agonising eternity.

In our hurry to leave the boat one of us had carelessly touched the chains. My mind ran riot with fear. Would they find us? Would they shoot before finding out who we were? We lay motionless on the ground hidden by tall grass similar to bulrushes. The thumping of our hearts seemed deafening as we listened for the sound of any footsteps or the barking of dogs. All was quiet. The lights went out, creating such a blackness we were unable to see each other.

We crept along the ground which was rough and boggy. We stumbled in the dark. Our boots filled with water making a squelching sound with each step. We ran into fences, fell full length into ditches and eventually exhausted gave up. Noname said dejectedly, 'It is useless to keep going. Man cannot walk in a straight line in the dark. Instinctively we go in circles. If we keep on going we will land back at the shore and probably into a sentry. As we have no idea where we are it is best to stay here until daylight. There is no moon to guide us.'

We lay down on the cold wet boggy grass until the dawn broke and we could distinguish the land and trees, then we slowly and cautiously moved on.

Our route took us through open country which meant we were constantly on the alert. We passed close to a farmhouse, walked across fields and reached a small hut used for sheltering cattle during bad weather. We longed for a place to hide and rest and sleep! Warily we approached the hut. There was no door, only an opening and we wondered if there were any animals inside. If there were cows we could huddle down beside them for warmth. We crept in feeling our way in the darkness. There were no animals, but there was some straw on the ground. How clean or dirty we would find out in the morning! Now it didn't matter!

We sat down. Noname advised us that our feet would stay warmer if we did not remove our boots, but that we should try and empty the water from them. We did so by raising our legs, but of course the water poured on to our already wet clothing. Shivering, exhausted and hungry we lay down and tried to sleep. When morning came we were still shivering and my feet were like ice. I tore up my vest, took off my boots and wet socks and wrapped my feet in the strips of cloth. I offered pieces to my companions. They were reluctant to accept at first, then gratefully took the cloth and wrapped it around their feet. I brought out my minute piece of bread roll, but they refused to take a crumb, saying I might be glad of it later.

We surveyed the surrounding countryside from the shelter, then cautiously crept out of the hut. Noname was afraid of being seen. I had been warned about wandering fugitives who through hunger and despera-tion were driven to robbing, beating up and even killing anyone for food or clothing. Noname's concern, however, was of being reported to the authorities. Breaking the imposed curfew was a serious offence, but it was more serious to be found without identity cards or permits and we had none. We travelled like fugitives across fields and through forests to avoid being seen. Noname was particularly afraid of the American zone. The American forces were the target of sabotage and were suspicious of any unregistered persons, or anyone acting suspiciously.

Moving by day we were able to establish our direction and walked towards the west. We avoided any roads, houses or farms. It was exhausting, trudging without food or drink across the open land, climbing high fences, clambering over stone walls, squeezing through barbed wire. We never relaxed and stress sapped our sagging energy. Ever vigilant we would hide if we saw anyone, and remain hidden until they had gone out of sight.

In time Stephen left us to travel south. I was dejected at his departure. During the brief time together we had become close, like a brother and sister, enduring near death situations. Now I would never see him again. We parted affectionately, promising to remember each other in our prayers.

Noname, an unusual companion
I was ill at ease travelling with Noname alone. He was a very unpleasant companion, and I began to consider a reason to leave him. I had become increasingly suspicious of him because of his attitude and obsession to avoid people. He never revealed his name; where he was born; or where he came from – only that he wanted to

cross the River Weser at a point much further to the south. My plans were to reach Westerstede as soon as possible and cross the Weser near Bremen which was a considerable distance to the north.

I found an opportunity to tell him and bade him goodbye wishing him a safe journey. I thought he would be glad to see the last of me. To my surprise he became very angry. His eyes sparked with such a fierce fury, that I drew back afraid that he would kill me if I went on my own way. It then dawned on me that this strange companion had all along been using me for his own ends. If challenged, at any time, he could say that we were a couple travelling together, or that we lived nearby.

He retorted, 'You do not know the way as all the bridges are blown up. I understand that the bridges in the north arc still standing.' Then as if to assure me, he said, 'It will be much safer for us to travel together. At least until we reach the Weser, where I will find some way to get you across. Besides the countryside is still very dangerous for a single girl. You are very young and we are still close to the battlefront!' I had no choice but to agree and I nodded my consent.

We sat talking, as we usually did, two or three yards apart. We were resting by a brook where we washed and drank some water. The sun was setting and we had nowhere to go.

Being near the battlefront we were under constant fear of being spotted and hurried further into the forest. The sound of a twig snapping startled us. We lay flat on the ground hardly daring to breathe. Someone, quietly and cautiously, was approaching. My heart thumped so loudly I feared it would be heard. I dared not look and prayed. The footsteps were close. I expected any moment to be discovered. A man's voice, hushed and reassuring called, 'It's alright! I am one of you!' Not daring to believe him I lay still until Noname acknowledged him and began a conversation.

The stranger was German and like ourselves fleeing from the Russians. He knew the area well and was able to give us useful information. He warned us about the many dangerous swamps in the forest that could suck you in like quicksands. He told us that there were army lookout towers erected at regular intervals along the main roads. Anyone seen near them was shot immediately.

Sitting listening to Noname and the stranger the dangers ahead began to dawn on me, for we had no alternative but to go that way. I was now certain that Noname was a German deserter, for whilst we had travelled for weeks in virtual silence, he sat animated talking to the stranger in a deep discussion. We were forewarned, however, and Noname knew what precautions to take. His knowledge and quick reaction had already saved our lives and I had to continue trusting him.

Noname spotted the army towers long before I did. The towers were of metal and concrete construction. Soldiers, with machine guns at the ready, looked out from each side. Noname explained that each tower had long distance observation equipment and we must keep well hidden, moving with caution from tree to tree. He studied the moss on the trees; knew which side it grew; knew when we would have neither moon, stars or sun to guide us. When criss-crossing the forest to avoid the swamps he knew how to keep on the right direction.

Eventually we had no alternative but to cross a main road close to lookout towers. We approached with caution. By making a wide detour into the forest we managed to avoid being seen from one of the towers and reached the roadside. Keeping close to the woods we sat down to rest and wait our chance to make a dash for it across the road. Suddenly, as if from nowhere, two American soldiers appeared.

'Who are you? What are you doing here? Where are you going,' they asked aggressively.

Noname had warned me that if ever we were caught I must never look startled. We must pretend to be a couple living nearby. He mumbled a name and waved in the direction behind him, saying, 'We live there!'

The soldiers gave us another look and then left us, saying, 'Get away from here and back home as fast as you can!'

We scurried away into the thicket and hid until it was dark. As we lay helicopters circled above. Occasionally bullets whistled through the woods, but we remained still and silent for our very lives depended on that.

When it was pitch dark and there was no sound of military activity Noname decided we should make another attempt to escape. This time we crossed the road unobserved. The night was bitterly cold for it was still winter. I became exhausted from creeping along the wet ground and struggling through dense thicket. Several times we had to turn back as the thicket was too dense to squeeze through. We became afraid of being trapped in the dense undergrowth in the dark and not finding our way out. Noname kept urging me on as I gradually lagged behind.

Then I fell exhausted to the ground unable to continue. I could see a few yards away a car tilted on its side and with a wheel missing. I called to Noname, 'Could we not rest in there for a while?' He replied, 'It would be foolish, cold and unsafe, especially if there was a thunder and lightning storm!'

He walked on. I looked plaintively at the black wreck. Suddenly I felt all alone. The car seemed to be a coffin; my surroundings a cemetery. Death was sitting opposite me, looking at me patiently without a flicker of eyelids. He seemed sure of his prey – *me*! Panic and terror swept over me. My heart pounded. A cold sweat poured down my face. Was I to perish here like a stray beast? My heart cried out in agony to God, 'Do you not care that I perish here?' I could see no way out and pleaded to God to do something. He had surely not brought me this far to die from exposure?

Hospitality denied

Suddenly the deathly silence was broken by the barking of a dog. I listened intently. Was it a delusion of an agonised mind? I could tell, quite clearly, the direction of the barking. To my utter amazement there was no echo! A forest and no echo! I struggled to my feet. 'There must be a farm and people near,' I thought. I moved in the direction of the barking. Noname appeared. I had thought he had deserted me but he had not gone far. The barking without an echo, puzzled him. 'Could it be dogs are hunting for us?' he asked, 'But then the dogs would stand and remain silent!'

With new hope and faith I pressed on clambering, through the bushes. Suddenly I could see traces of a forest path. 'A path! A path!' I shouted excitedly, 'It must lead somewhere!' With our eyes fixed to the tracks because of the increasing darkness we followed them until we came to a clearing, and then later on a cluster of farmsteads. 'Let us beg for shelter and food!' I said, but Noname remained in the shadows. 'You go!' he agreed at last. I did.

Careful not to startle a dog or run into unpleasant company I approached a farmhouse, but my pleadings were refused. How many others I tried I cannot recall but the answer was always the same, 'No. Go away!' Passing the comfortable homes and straw-filled barns awoke in me a longing for a warm and dry place to rest. 'Let us make sure that there is a barn with straw at the next house we try!' I suggested, 'Surely they just could not refuse!'

We found one. I knocked at the door. A man opened it, his dark frame silhouetted against the warm lit room. The room looked so cosy and inviting. I asked, 'Sir, we seek your help and kindness. May we have a drink of cold water and permission to shelter in your barn?' I was so sure he would not refuse! If someone came to our farm in Poland with such a request we invited them in, gave them warm milk and bread and a place to sleep by the kitchen fire. I had asked for nothing more than cold water and to sleep on the straw in the barn.

The man looked me up and down several times whilst I spoke. When I had finished he said coldly, 'No!' I pleaded with him but this made him angry and, waving his arm, he shouted, 'You get back to where you came from. All the way to Poland!' His threatening anger terrified me as he chased me down the path as one would chase an unwelcome dog. 'If you do not clear out of here at once I shall report you to the police. They will know what to do with your kind. If I find any trace of you around here any time I shall do so!' I fled like a beaten animal, too hurt to weep!

I longed for a place to rest and would not give up trying. Desperation drove me to knock on another farmstead door. The door opened and two young women stood in a well lit hallway. I pleaded for shelter. They hesitated, then pointing to a brick-built barn, one said, 'You can go in there. It has an attic with two bedsteads, and there is straw on the wooden bases. Soldiers slept there. We must warn you that there are large gaping holes in the walls caused by explosions. The soldiers hung sacking in front of them so most of the holes are covered up.'

I thanked them and then dared to ask for a crust of bread. 'We are starving and thirsty. Please, could we have some water and a crust of bread? It does not matter how stale the bread is!' One of the women fetched a slice from the end of a loaf and I clutched it eagerly, thanking them profusely.

The attic was cold and dark. There were two double bedsteads in opposite corners. Two large gaping holes, the size of a door, were partially covered with sacking. A chill wind blew through the sacking and the sound of the flapping was eerie and nerve-racking. It was mid-winter and bitterly cold, but at least we had shelter and some dry straw to lie on. My body was like ice and I would not have minded lying close to another human being to stop my body shivering. After all, on my journeys I had frequently huddled close to men, women and children for warmth to survive. I could hear Noname shivering with cold, too, but he lay without speaking trying to sleep. We knew that each other was suffering.

As I lay awake I tried to understand why the people were so inhospitable. Perhaps they were afraid that we would stay, for who would want to be burdened with foreigners when there was not enough food, money or work for all. I lay dwelling on the suffering of the world, and the passionate tears of the child that I was froze on my cheeks. Not only was I cold but I was desperately hungry.

When dawn was beginning to break we got up, shared the crust of bread and left before anyone was about. We continued westwards keeping to the shelter of the woods close to the main roads. I was still very weak, and Noname became more gentle. We rested more often, whenever possible near a brook to wash and drink the clear water. Noname said, 'Once it is dark we could steal into a village and beg for shelter. We shall have a better chance together, for people suspect a person who is travelling alone.' I had no choice but to agree.

As soon as it was dark we walked into the village. There was a strict blackout and curfew in force and so we kept in the shadow of the buildings. We approached house after house but continued to be refused. By the time we reached the outskirts of the village I was tired and dejected and suggested returning to the woods. Ahead of us, standing in beautiful grounds, was a large imposing villa. Dared we go and ask? We looked at each other questioningly. Desperation drove us to make one last attempt.

In trepidation we entered the gates and walked up the drive. To our utter surprise the door opened and a pleasant faced motherly woman invited us in. We were awestruck! Her husband and daughter welcomed us. It was like a long awaited dream – a miracle! We were allowed to wash and then the daughter brought us coffee, bread and cheese. We told our hosts that we were not married, just two people meeting by chance and travelling in the same direction. We were given separate accommodation.

Our hosts told us that they had a son in the German army. They did not know whether he was dead or alive, but hoped and prayed that he was safe and being cared for by altruistic people. They were kind, compassionate people. I plucked up courage to ask if I could have a bath. The parents were reluctant, saying that they did not have hot water, and it was inadvisable to bathe in cold water in an unheated room in winter. I can still recall their tender, well-meaning faces and the daughter's large brown eyes staring at me in disbelief when I said, 'My body longs for a wash and I don't mind how cold the water is!'

The luxury of the bathroom, the large clean towel and clean water remains vividly in my memory. Whilst I soaked and scrubbed my body I contemplated how always when I was at the end of endurance and felt death near, something or someone came to strengthen me. I thanked God for his ever-loving care.

The home was indeed a haven of rest and love, such as one always hoped for but dared not expect.

We regretted leaving next morning but we knew we must move on without delay. It was good, however, to continue our journey, having slept in a comfortable bed and being given food and a hot drink to sustain us before leaving. We felt good to be alive. We thanked our hosts and wished them well.

Sharing a bicycle

The morning was beautiful. The sun shone sparkling on the snow covered landscape. Now it was daylight we could see that we had stayed in a large guesthouse. Adjacent to the house and grounds was a building with rows of bicycles parked in front of it. There must have been a hundred or more.

I turned to the husband, 'Why are there so many bicycles stacked together? Who do they belong to?'

He replied, 'They do not belong to anyone in particular. When the German army retreated they left them here. Displaced persons, such as yourself, have confiscated them to help them on their way. A number of refugees took refuge in the building to await the end of the war and until they could return home. I suppose it is a kind of displaced persons' camp!'

'It would be so much quicker to travel by bike than walking!' I said.

The man shrugged his shoulders and replied, 'There are certainly plenty of bikes and more where they came from, but you must take care not to be seen taking them. The crowd here are in a desperate and dangerous mood!'

Noname refused to go near the bikes, but I felt justified in taking one. After all, someone must have mine, and I was also a displaced person. My host returned to the house and closed the door. I walked to the pile of bikes, took the nearest one and left.

The road ahead was straight and stretched for miles into the horizon. There was no-one in sight. I pushed the bike, for Noname fiercely objected to me riding on it. He held on to the saddle determined to prevent me. I was greatly tempted to ride off and leave him, but somehow I felt that I owed him thanks, for without his help I would not have crossed the Elbe or come this far on my journey. On the other hand his aggressive attitude unnerved me and I was afraid to attempt an escape less I failed and suffered his revenge.

We walked on. He was such depressing company. Never smiling. Sometimes he would acknowledge my conversation with a nod, a shrug or just look blank. It was not that he was unintelligent or inarticulate. One glance was enough to tell me what he was thinking. I knew he was wondering if I would ride off and leave him, especially when I suggested that we take turns to ride the bike.

'One would ride on,' I said, 'later lay the bike down by the side of the road and walk on. The one following would pick up the bike, pass the one walking and then after a time, lay down the bike for the other to pick up and walk on. Like a relay.'

Noname looked at me with suspicion. I was angry that he did not have the courage to say what he was thinking.

I said, 'Why didn't you take a bike? Why should I walk for days just because of you?'

He didn't answer. I regretted my outburst and thought that perhaps it was integrity, not cowardice, that stopped him. If this was so, then he was more honest than me. I was, however, by this time determined to ride the bike. I rode off calling, 'I will not ride away!' I had expected Noname to stop me, but he surprised me by calling, 'Don't leave me!' After riding some distance I left the bike and walked on.

Now it was Noname's turn. He rode by without a glance. I panicked, suspicion filling my mind. Suppose he rode off! I was so weak I knew I could not make the journey on foot alone. The road seemed unending and there were no farms or houses to be seen. Shaking with fear I watched Noname cycle on and on. In time I saw him stop, lay down the bike and without a backward glance to see if I was coming walk on. I sighed with relief, calmed down and felt happier again.

We made good progress. The distances covered became greater and greater. Only when we were both completely exhausted did we stop. We would leave the road, look for a stream and rest there, drinking the water and washing our face, hands and feet. It was obvious that soon we would go our separate ways.

As we sat by a brook, as usual yards apart, I tried to get Noname to talk about himself. 'If your home is nearer than my parents' place, I would not refuse a wash and somewhere to sleep. I am also very hungry.' He did not reply, but sat with his head bent.

Earlier when I suggested we make towards Bremen he was adamant that we avoid it, saying, 'There will be British military in that area. I will go south. Nienburg will be a more likely place for you to cross the Weser!' So we went that way.

As time went on we found the people less suspicious.

At the roadside, near large farms, were large milk churns. We grew curious and decided to investigate. What joy! They contained fresh milk. On the side was a ladle and cup. No one was in sight. It was obvious that they had been put there to refresh weary travellers like ourselves. It was unbelievable! Then I remembered that my parents gave milk to the villagers and anyone in need when it could not be sold during the occupation. We drank to our content, savouring every mouthful. It was so good, nourishing and it also quenched our thirst. We found containers in several places and I thanked God for such kind-hearted people.

We were approaching the outskirts of Nienburg and I felt more optimistic. The city had escaped with little damage. The fighting had ceased. Everyone was more relaxed. People walked in the streets. When Noname saw the presence of the British army, he quickly left me.

Protection or Death!
I was now less afraid of being seen. I knew a few English phrases and felt sure I would be allowed to cross the Weser, a river I soon realised notorious for its treacherous currents.

The bridge over the river had been destroyed by the Germans. British engineers had replaced it with a floating bridge of boats and planks. As this temporary construction could only support traffic crossing from one side at a time, control centres linked by telephone were placed at each end of the bridge. Each were manned by an army officer and some soldiers.

I walked confidently towards the bridge. Large queues had formed. Most of the traffic consisted of military personnel and vehicles, but there were a number of horse-drawn carts and pedestrians. I could see civilians produce a permit or kind of passport. Every document was carefully scrutinised. I had no papers, but I did not give up hope. I approached the guards and explained my position. 'I am a Polish refugee. I was abducted by the Germans during the occupation and sent to a labour camp. Now I want to find my parents in Westerstede.' They listened attentively and I was taken to see the officer standing by the telephone control box.

I was optimistic, so confident that a young girl, although weather-beaten and grubby, could persuade a British gentleman with her manners and knowledge of English. My first English lesson from Papa had been taken from the book *Little Lord Fountleroy*, and so my perception of an Englishman was based on this.

The officer treated me with the utmost courtesy. He was under very great pressure and the telephone line kept ringing, but he took time to listen to me. Anxious, I am sure, not to hurt my feelings he said kindly, 'If I could put you in my pocket and carry you across I would do so. I am indeed sorry that I cannot help you, but I am under strict orders not to let anyone across without a permit or registration document, and you have neither.' I was devastated, but thanked him as I walked away not knowing where to go or what to do!

Wandering through the strange city, I must have looked dejected and forlorn, for I was again at my wits' end. I was weary, hungry and depressed. It was gathering dusk. I dragged my aching body leaning heavily on the bike. I knew I could not remain unnoticed, for I stuck out like a sore thumb, but there was nothing I could do.

If the forests brought a sense of utter isolation, the city with its many buildings and myriad of streets was confusing. In an open field a hole could often be found, but in a city of brick walls, paving stones and asphalt, one could not sit down and rest without being noticed. I sank down on a pavement in utter despair.

Suddenly a hand fell on my shoulder. Startled I turned round expecting someone in authority ready to apprehend me. I looked into the face of a kindly elderly lady.

'Are you lost, my dear?' she enquired. 'It is curfew time and you will have to leave the streets.'

Had she sensed my distress? Had God guided her to me? I stared in disbelief and could not answer. I did not ask for help, but this unknown woman invited me to her home. She took me to her flat in the city, gave me warm water to wash my whole body and I swilled out my socks and underwear. With food, drink and a place to sleep I was comforted and at peace and fell into a deep sleep.

I woke up refreshed. With renewed strength and faith I was more than ever determined to reach my parents. I confided in my new friend that as I could not cross the river by bridge I would swim across. She begged me not to do so, saying, 'That would be very unwise. The Weser has dangerous currents and you could be swept away. It is also forbidden to cross without a permit and there are armed soldiers continually guarding the river banks on both sides. They will shoot at anyone trying to swim across.'

She could not dissuade me, and realising how determined I was she told me where to cross to avoid the treacherous currents and whirlpools. 'Hide on the right side of the bridge,' she advised, 'Then when the coast is clear swim out under the shadow of the bridge!'

I shall never forget that day. The sun shone. It was the 3rd of May, 1945, my brother Eugene's birthday. I wondered where he was. Was he safe or a prisoner of war?

We had always celebrated family birthdays, although they were humble affairs. Presents were usually something we had made ourselves. My last gift to Eugene was a pair of book ends. The last birthday we celebrated as a family was Mama's. Unknown to Mama we decorated the living room with dozens of yellow flowers and Papa hung a floral wall hanging. When our gifts were laid on the table we called Mama in and sang 'Happy Birthday'. I had composed a tune for her and when I played it on the violin she wept copiously. Recollections of such memories touched me deeply. I was so homesick and longed to see my family and searching for them took on a new desperate urgency.

I said goodbye to my new found friend. It was an emotional parting for she had given me food, shelter and love when I needed it so much. I did not want to part with my bike, for it had served me well and if I were to reach Westerstede I would need it. I still had some distance to cover.

Approaching the bridge, I could see the sentries, guns slung over their shoulder, marching up and down the river bank. A considerable line of traffic had formed waiting to cross the bridge. I noticed a kindly farmer with an empty horse-drawn cart and approached him. 'Please, sir, could you take me across in your cart?' He assured me that he had a pass for only one person and goods. I begged him to take my bike and although puzzled at the request he agreed. It was arranged that he would take my bike to his farm which was five miles from the crossing, and I would pick it up there.

Taking great care not to be noticed I climbed down underneath the remains of the old bridge to where the river was wide and calm. I knew I could not swim fast, but I could keep afloat for at least an hour. But what about my clothing? It was too cold to walk in dripping wet clothes.

Two boys were playing under the arch of the old bridge with an empty petrol can and having fun pulling it about in the water like a boat. It gave me an idea! The petrol cans could be used to carry my clothes across! I asked the boys to fish out some petrol cans conveniently tied together. They looked at me as if I was crazy, but did so.

When there was no-one about I stripped off my outer clothes and tied them neatly onto the petrol cans and launched out into the river. It was difficult pushing the cans and balancing them in order to keep my clothes from getting soaked. I seemed to be making good progress when suddenly I was caught in a strong undercurrent. The water sucked me down and pulled me back to the shore. As I struggled for my life I could see on the river bank the sentry from whom I had hid. I was now in grave danger of being spotted and shot at, or becoming another victim of this treacherous river with its many dangerous whirlpools.

My strength suddenly drained. Reaching the other shore was now beyond my capabilities. I felt doomed. As I was swept down with the current I could see that the problem was caused by a bend in the river. I cried out to God to help me and he heard. I was given enough strength to struggle on. I redoubled my efforts. Eventually, exhausted but triumphant, I reached the other shore. I dragged my body on to the bank and lay on the grass gasping for breath. I thanked God for once more hearing my cry when faced with death, and saving me.

Even in my near-death situation I had been aware that I needed my clothing and clung desperately to the petrol cans. When I had recovered sufficiently I pulled on my dress and raincoat (which the Dutch captain's wife had given me) over my wet underclothes and went in search of the farm and my bike. I was exuberant. Surely now nothing could stop me from finding my family.

But I still had a long way to go.

6

Journey's End
June 1945-1947

United and Free!

The country west of the Weser was pastoral and flat with well scattered farms which had suffered little from the war. Long drives leading to the farmhouses made the search for the bicycle confusing and tiring. It was still dangerous for a girl to be travelling alone in such isolated places and I sought cover whenever I saw anyone. My past traumatic experiences had now made me extremely nervous and I was terrified when passing close to bushes or trees, expecting someone to pounce out on me. I was tired and weak. The road, stretching on into the far horizon, seemed to mock me and I walked on with little enthusiasm.

It was gathering dusk and beginning to drizzle when I heard the rumble of a cart behind me. I panicked and wondered if I should hide. Yet something prompted me to stay put. As the sound grew nearer I looked back and saw a horse-drawn cart being driven by an elderly gentleman with a kindly face, a long grey beard and twinkling eyes. He hailed me, 'Girl, what are you doing walking alone so far from a village on such a night?' I felt I could trust him and told him. He knew the farm, and with gratitude and relief I accepted his offer of a lift.

In time we came to the farm. The farmer's wife was surprised to see me, for although her husband had brought my bike as he promised, they both feared that I would not be able to cross the River Weser. She gave me some milk and bread and whilst I ate she gave me directions to Westerstede. She begged me to rest and set off at dawn, but I was now too restless and anxious to find my family. I thanked her and rode on.

My determination to reach Westerstede surpassed my strength and I soon tired. It was getting too dark to cycle without lights and I needed to rest. Plucking up courage I left the road and took shelter in a copse. The rain had stopped by now and the night sky was studded with stars. I lay down on the moss and grass. It was sweet-smelling and soft. I felt at peace.

Watching the stars twinkle and the soft clouds drift by, just as Eugene and I did when so very young, I became aware of God as the Creator. This was the home of my Father in Heaven. He had made me. I was part of his creation. He had kept me safe and I knew he would continue to do so. My fears subsided and a soothing calm swept over me. For the first time since being abducted from Poland I had time to gaze in wonder and meditate .... Was the war over? Peace in the world would be so good!

I emerged from the copse at daybreak. My clothes had partially dried overnight and now astride my bike I took to the road. The days and nights went by in a new tranquillity, as if the earth had been resurrected. I continued to travel alone seeking the shelter of forests and copses although I no longer felt I had to hide. There was no evidence of fighting and an inner peace glowed within me.

In time I began to see signposts for Westerstede and Felde. Surely nothing could stop me now! I prayed that my family was safe and that nothing would prevent me from being reunited. With mixed feelings of elation and apprehension, I rode through the city suburbs and on to the main arterial road. The pavements were crowded with people, but this time I didn't care.

It never occurred to me that I could be singled out in a busy thoroughfare! I was aware of my unkempt appearance – my battered old bike and the fact that I was wearing a plastic coat on a hot sunny day. I wore old army boots on bare legs. Before entering the city, however, I had stopped at a brook to wash my face, my feet, my hair and boots, so felt reasonably clean. Indeed, there were very few reasonably dressed persons to be seen.

Imagine my surprise then, when someone called out to me, 'Are you the daughter of Mr Pladek?' I stopped and answered, 'Yes, I am.' The stranger continued, 'I am a second cousin. Every day your Papa stands out on the road looking for you and your brother!' He gave me directions. Only another two miles and I should see my family! It seemed too good to be true and I rode on forgetting my tiredness in my excitement to be reunited.

Soon I could see a lone figure standing in the middle of the road. As I approached he walked towards me. It was Papa! He gathered me up in his arms and we wept and wept. No words were spoken for a long time, then he told me how he stood for hours each day looking for Eugene and me. 'God has answered our prayers, Nina.

I have heard that Eugene is alive. I shall continue to wait on the road until he returns too.'

'Bless Papa,' I thought. 'He is such a caring and loving father.'

Papa led me into farm buildings which comprised a barn, stables and a pigsty. We walked over a threshing floor to the far end where a large open fire threw out a grey ashy smoke. On either side of the fire were the living quarters with floors made of hard clay. One space was the kitchen area served by an iron stove. A small wooden table stood on stone slabs. The living area had a partial wooden floor and there, sorting out clothes, stood Mama. She gave out a shriek of delight; ran towards me and throwing her arms around me, burst into tears. Theodore, my baby brother just stared and gave me a shy glance. I was now a total stranger to him. He ran out into the yard before I could hug him. He was now nearly six years old. The baby I had brought up when Mama was so ill did not know me. (The long separation, and changed circumstances affected our relationship. I loved him dearly; would do anything for him, but the estrangement continued.)

Papa turned to me, 'Your homecoming, Nina, is like the arrival of an angel. It comforts your mother. She has cried constantly for you. Now she can stop grieving for we now know that Eugene is alive.'

When Eugene was abducted by the Germans he was barely fifteen years old. Mama and Papa did not know what had become of him and prayed continually that he was alive. Papa never gave up trying to discover Eugene's whereabouts and eventually was able to trace him through the British army.

Eugene was forced to join the German army, but when he was captured and later liberated by the British he was sent to Scotland and joined the Polish forces. His detachment fought with the British army in Holland and into Northern Germany. By a strange coincidence the army's route was through the village of Felde. Eugene was not aware that our family was there.

Papa stood out on the road from dawn to dusk, day after day, always hoping, always believing with his enduring faith that his son would pass by.

The British contingent began to arrive, and for days Papa stood scanning the faces of the troops. It was 5am when his vigil was eventually rewarded. Advancing with a group of Polish soldiers, guns at the ready, Papa recognised the weather-beaten face of a young soldier. It was Eugene, now matured into a handsome young man! As Papa told me tears ran down his face and his voice broke with deep sobs. How can words describe the joyous turmoil of a devoted father's reactions, or the frustration of a father and son seeing each other after such a long and forced separation, and not being able to embrace? Eugene and Papa could merely acknowledge each other. Papa shouted out the name of the village and pointed to the farm buildings. They knew now that each was alive and that soon they would be reunited.

Mama and Papa wanted to know what had happened to me since we lost each other in the flight from Poland. When I had finished my story Papa told me theirs.

'When you left us in Pabjanice to cross the road, Nina, we were held up for hours by numerous accidents. Driven by desperation and fear, people took risks crossing the snow-covered main roads already congested with the retreating German armies. Carts were hit and overturned, scattering their loads in the path of the fleeing hordes. In the chaos and panic many people lost their few belongings and several were killed or badly injured. There were no facilities to remove the dead or treat the injured. In such appalling winter conditions, I doubt if the badly injured could survive. We did what we could to help and found ourselves trapped in the endless stream of panic-stricken refugees.

'The Russians were gaining on us, and time was running out. I could not risk the family being captured and had somehow to go on. When an opportunity came we fled across the frozen fields. We were heartbroken at losing you, but remembering your promise to return to the labour camp and your description of where it was, we vowed that we would risk looking for you.

'The days and nights in an open cart began to affect little Theo. He was a brave little boy never complaining, even when frozen and hungry. When any food or drink dribbled down his face or neck it would freeze and stick to his clothing, making him colder and uncomfortable.

'Felix insisted on trying to get milk for Theo and often risked losing us when trudging through the snow-covered fields to a farm. But our prayers were answered. We were one of the few who survived and we are still together.

'Every time we saw any army tank tracks in the snow we would deviate onto them and I was able to drive the horses faster. We slept in deserted farms or barns where we often found food and water for the horses. The urgency to reach western Germany was such that there was no time to stop and rest during the day. We had to keep moving when the refugee and army traffic would allow it. Several times we were stopped by German officials and sent back. I would plead with them or try to force a way through, but we had to turn back. If I found another road I took it. After deviating towards Berlin and finding you, we were happier and uplifted finding new courage to continue to Westerstede.

'I had lost touch with my sister over the years and we did not know what her circumstances were. Sadly her husband was the innocent victim of a shooting incident, and shortly afterwards your aunt died of a broken heart.

'Her daughter, your cousin Maria, took us into her home. She knew of an elderly widower in Felde who needed some help on the farm, and here we are. As you can see it is a small farm, where we tend the land and care for the livestock. In return we have our food and accommodation in the barn. It is common in this part of Germany to have labourers' living space in the barn. We sleep under the sloping roof. The kitchen is in a shed. Felix has proved a wonderful and kind son. He works hard and has taken on all the farm labouring.'

Mama interjected, and in a voice which threatened to break down, said, 'Oh Nina, it is not like our lovely farmhouse in Poland, but we are thankful to have a roof over our heads. The cows are tied to one side of the barn; on the other side is the pigsty. We cook on an old iron stove with peat. When the wind blows, which it does most days, the place is covered in a fine grey ash. The place is so cold and damp, and we try to dry the mattresses when we can. But, you are with us now and we have a place to live together. We will soon make it a home again!'

A family again

It was July, 1945. Two months after Papa saw him Eugene came home on leave. Our reunion was such an emotional one. Now Mama could really stop grieving! We were a family again. Felix had helped Papa on the land and we would also do our bit! I resolved to do all I could to help my ailing parents and tackled any task, even the ones I disliked, like cleaning the pigsty. I have always been sensitive to bad smells and the stench from the pigsty made me vomit, but by going out often for fresh air I was able to complete the task.

I handled the plough; drove the sowing and harrowing machinery; worked the harvester; and milked the cows by hand. When neighbouring farmers were short of labour during the haymaking and harvest time we helped them. Papa still had the horses he had brought from Poland, and as they knew me this helped greatly, for I was still weak and tired very easily.

I had no clothes. When I returned home and washed my clothing they disintegrated immediately. Sweat and dirt had held them together. As I looked at the filthy mulch I realised that without the plastic coat, which the Dutch captain's wife had given me, I might have been naked! I shuddered at the thought! Mama took me to a clothing distribution centre in Westerstede that was run by the American Red Cross. I was given a dress, jacket and a pair of canvas shoes with wooden soles. I had no stockings. We were also given some woollen garments and as they were unsuitable Mama and I unravelled them and knitted colourful jumpers and cardigans for the family. Knitting needles were unobtainable and Papa made some from the wheel spokes of an old bike.

Gradually we tried to settle into our new life in West Germany. It wasn't easy. The brutal Nazi regime had taken its toll on all our lives. When Eugene and I were abducted from home we were schoolchildren – now we were adults. We had been robbed of our youth, thrown among hostile adults and forced to behave in a manner contrary to our Christian upbringing. God had been good. He had reunited us with our family. With their love my parents tried to smooth away our sufferings, but the deep wounds remained. I had always been a delicate child and small for my age. I was prone to sleepwalking as a child, which more than once nearly led to my death. Now I suffered terrible nightmares. Eugene continued to return home on short visits until he returned to Scotland with the Polish forces.

Papa was more disabled and unable to do heavy farm work. It was heartbreaking to see him retire into a less active role. Papa was the embodiment of his race – courageous, humbly heroic, gentle and honest, with his heart deeply rooted in his family and the regenerating earth – the Phoenix qualities of the Polish nation. He was a casualty of man's godlessness – once again exiled from his homeland and robbed of his farm and home – finishing his life labouring for a German farmer. Mama found a new strength in her adversity and never ceased to strive to improve our home surroundings.

The family became more and more involved in the local Baptist church which was the pulse of our community. The minister, Mark, was young and keen, and cared deeply for his congregation. With his wife and baby daughter he had fled from Berlin and now had nothing. He was shot through the knee, whilst serving in the German army, and walked with a stiff leg. To visit his much scattered congregation, he cycled whenever he could by pedalling his bike with one foot.

Mark was especially good with young people and his youth fellowship meetings were well attended. The German farming community spoke openly about their faith, but few attended church regularly. The young people who attended church were mostly from the town of Westerstede. Mark tried to foster friendly relations with the youth. At social functions I always felt an outcast. If any boys showed an interest in me, the parents quickly stopped it, for they did not want a poor Polish refugee in their family. I never revealed that I had no wish to settle in Germany.

The years of malnourishment with the added sufferings and trauma of my flight across Germany had seriously affected my health. Working in the fields in bare feet during bitterly cold and windy weather caused my legs to break out in boils. I had no bandages or medicine to treat them and they continued to fester. Any exertion made the boils burst open and this delayed their healing.

Felix and I had the job of providing the peat needed for cooking and heating. My condition worsened and I found it exhausting work. The wet peat was heavy. It lay beneath layers of grass which had to be removed before you could begin cutting it into neat, manageable clods suitable for stacking and burning. The air had to be able to circulate around each clod. We took turns to climb into the pit, cut and lift out the peat, whilst the other loaded up the horse-drawn trailer (rather like a large sledge). The peat was then unloaded in a field some distance away, where it was stacked for drying. When dry the clods were lighter and easier to handle and were then brought home by cart.

I had been at home a year when our cousin, Paul, visited us. He was partially sighted and the last surviving member of Aunt Martha's family. He had started shoe-making and now had plans to open a shoe factory. He begged my parents to let me help him. His excuse was that the shoe factory would not only provide income for his family, but give others an opportunity to work and earn a living.

There was a great need and demand for shoes and slippers in the postwar years. Paul knew where he could obtain discarded camouflage tent material. He made the project sound so attractive. Whilst working there I would be able to earn enough money to live on and buy things, such as clothes which I needed badly. It seemed a sound proposition. Felix agreed to do my work on the farm so that I could go. The move to a town seemed a welcome change and I accepted the offer for a trial period only.

Dangerous encounters

The expectations of an easier and more pleasant life after the drudgery of farm work gave me a new lease of life. I was fond of my cousin and his family and we shared the same love of music. I would be helping others and for the first time I would be earning a living.

Dreams and the reality, however, are seldom alike. Sometimes my head and stomach ached from hunger. My cousins were not unkind to me. We all ate together, but food was rationed and scarce in the city. I had to work hard for long hours, and had not expected to continue working every night, turning by hand a 'Heath Robinson' type of contraption which was fitted with a wire brush. Paul pressed rubber soles, already cut to size on to the sharp wires, whilst I turned the handle for hours on end. The wires roughened the sole, enabling a rubber solution to stick onto the uppers.

During the day I had to sew the uppers. When a sufficient supply of the uppers and soles were ready I nailed uppers, insoles and soles together. This was done by putting a dozen or so nails in my mouth. Using my tongue I pushed a nail so that it came out head first. Forceps were used to grip the nail, push it into the uppers and soles, and then holding the pieces firmly in place I hammered in the nail. Finally the sole which had been roughened the previous evening was stuck on.

In time I made myself a pair of sandals with canvas uppers and cork soles, and a pair of shoes for Theodore. Later we made and sold canvas baby shoes. Every article had to be registered and a tax paid.

It was a joy to see the happiness of people being able to purchase footwear. Material was in short supply and some customers brought their own. It was a case of trial and error. Mostly we were successful, but sometimes shoes had to be remade or repaired free of charge. Too much glue made the soles too stiff and the uppers tore away.

My relaxation was found at the local Christian fellowship meetings. I became a Sunday School teacher and joined the choir. There were many refugees and I felt at home among them. We met in the home of a widow and her daughter, Anna, with whom I had become friendly. Their house was large and isolated and they were delighted to have company. Paul formed a music group and soon had a quartet, comprising of two violins (Paul was lead violin), a cello and piano. Paul often gave violin recitals and was sometimes accompanied by Anna on the piano. We loved these occasions, which were all too rare because of the long hours we worked at the factory.

The effects of war on the people was so apparent. War is so destructive. It is like a volcanic eruption burning, destroying not only the earth, but taking every creature with it. Man is tossed, thrown, separated and wounded in body and soul. The aftermath of war is terrifying, and more far-reaching than physical pain, starvation, disease and death. It penetrates into the very depths of the heart and mind.

Circumstances too often bring out the worst features in humanity. Moral standards are lowered. People become so accustomed to corruption and promiscuity that they grow lethargic and accept the situation rather than taking action to improve it. The strain of living under constant relentless pressure and oppression takes over part of the sub-conscience.

The wartime years of my childhood and youth had been lived under constant fear and the terrible nightmares began to haunt me by day. The same dream would recur. I would be drowning in the sea and struggling helplessly whilst a stranger held me down. I woke up terrified and bathed in perspiration. Struggling in prayer, I beseeched God to take the nightmares away.

The daytime brought other problems and my heart ached when I witnessed the human tragedies surrounding me. In Ecclesiastes we are told, 'There is a time to weep and a time to laugh'. I was still living in the time to weep and longed for a time to laugh.

I befriended a young woman who worked in the factory. She never smiled and seemed to grow more and more depressed. One day, she confided in me that she had been raped by several Russian soldiers. She gave birth to a son. 'An ugly, bad tempered beast', is how she described the child. 'Was the child really like that or the product of her hurt mind?' I wondered. 'The child, a constant reminder of her chilling experience.' I tried to help her but felt so inadequate, as I often did in such circumstances.

How could I tell her that one needs to take time and have the courage to think calmly on one's past experiences and deal with them in the light of God's Word, so that we may not only learn from them, but be morally and spiritually strengthened, trusting in God to show us an answer at a later date. If one has a sense of guilt, or shame, then accept God's forgiveness and the knowledge that it is impossible to go through life with conviction and certainty that every word spoken, every decision made, will be perfect.

I had come to Paul's workshop on the clear understanding that it would be for a trial period only. Paul was now most anxious that I should stay. I was, however, ill and losing weight and longed to be back surrounded by the love of my family. My cousin consented to give me leave of absence and paid me a bonus of 50 marks, which was equal to several weeks wages.

I travelled home by train, a journey that was neither pleasant nor reliable. One was never sure of getting a connection; or when and where to change trains, for the military authorities always had priority. The journeys were not only hazardous, but dangerous for lone passengers, especially girls, which I found to my cost.

When travellers obtained a pass and purchased a ticket to a given destination they were not permitted to leave any station en route until the destination was reached. They had to leave the train when ordered to do so; wait for their connection – sometimes all night. At night the station gates were locked and guarded. Passengers, men, women and children crowded down on the floor of the waiting room and tried to sleep. I was settling down when a voice shouted out, 'Anyone going to Hanover can get a lift there now, for we do not know when the next train will arrive.' Passengers scrambled to their feet. I followed them to the exit door. There was jostling and shouting. Passports were demanded.

A man in uniform produced papers and said he was allowed to take passengers. In the semi-darkness of the dimly lit station, he grabbed me by the arm and pulled me through the gate past the protesting railway guard. I looked round. There was no-one else following. The other passengers were left behind. I protested and asked, 'Where are the others?' 'Oh, never mind them! I could only get one of you past the guard!' was the reply. I was alarmed and doubted his sincerity. In a gentle voice, the stranger explained, 'I thought I might as well give someone a lift as the train service is so bad and I am travelling in the same direction.'

He then persuaded me to drive the car. I had never driven one before, and was taken aback at the request. I thought he must be tired of driving. 'The roads are clear and you only have to steer straight ahead!' I took the wheel and, although in some trepidation, I enjoyed the experience. Then, it happened! I steered the car straight into a ditch! The man swore, turned the wheel round, and took over the driving. I had presumed that steering a car was similar to riding a bike and had turned the wheel in the wrong direction.

We drove on until we came to a quiet country road. The man turned the car on to a forest path. I protested, 'I want to keep going! I might as well have waited for the train!' Only then did I realise the man's ulterior motive, and why he had grabbed me and taken no other passengers! In previous circumstances terror had paralysed me. This time a stubborn, determined anger possessed me.

The man grabbed me and I fought back like a mad wild animal. I bit him! I clawed him with my nails! I screamed and shouted abuse at him for deceiving me. I had never at any time displayed such angry passion. It was as if all the pent-up anger and disgust I had felt when attacked by the Russians and Germans was unleashed and bursting out uncontrolled.

It was amazing that the man did not go berserk on me, and hit back. Physically he was stronger and could have so easily overpowered me. My fury continued and in the end he let go of me, and unbelievably fell asleep. Only then did I realise that he had been drinking alcohol. What was a curse for some, this time probably saved me and was a blessing in disguise!

I stayed awake and alert during the night, letting the stranger sleep. As soon as it was light I tried to wake him. I was very cold and still angry with the stranger, and also myself for having been led into this situation. It took time and effort to wake him. At first he had no idea where he was or what had happened. I ordered him to get driving and like a lamb he obeyed. I thanked God for once more escaping from a sexual attack unscathed except for a few bruises.

Some months later I set off for Hamburg to see the British consulate, for I still hoped to make my home in Britain. Trains were still infrequent and unreliable. I arrived in Hamburg too late to be seen by anyone and made an appointment for the next day. This entailed having to spend the night in the city. I had no money, and knew no-one where I might seek hospitality. I had no alternative but to return to the station. I approached the station master and asked whether I could spend the night in the waiting room. He hesitated saying, 'There is no-one else waiting for a train at this time. It may be dangerous for you being on your own.'

As he spoke a man approached and said, 'I know where you can spend the night! My mother is a widow. My sister lives with her and they often take in people who are stranded. They are really kind-hearted and I am sure would give you supper as well.' He was well-dressed and looked respectable. I believed him and gratefully accepted. We drove to the house and he asked me to wait in, what appeared to be, a garden summer-house. I noticed that it contained two beds. The man said, 'Wait until I tell my mother that you are here. There is a swimming pool. You can have a swim.'

The pool looked inviting with the reflection of the

full moon dancing on the water. I loved swimming and accepted. A few minutes after I had returned from the pool and was fully dressed, the man reappeared, stepped into the room and locked the door. I was taken aback and gasped in astonishment. I panicked! How could I have been such a fool! Noticing my reaction, he tried to appease me by offering me some apples. So this was my supper! I tried to scream, but no sound came. The summerhouse stood in large gardens and was so isolated from the house it is doubtful if anyone would have heard me calling for help. I tried to get out, but the windows and door were firmly locked.

The man tried to calm me, insisting that there were two beds and a partition between them. He undressed and went into one of the beds. 'You can do the same, unless you want to stand up all night, for I have no intention of unlocking the door!' He was tall, young and well built. I was scared! I called him a cheat and a selfish brute. It then dawned on me that I did not know his name. I could not recall seeing the name of the road, or number or name of the house. If I did escape I had no idea which way to run.

A feeling of resentment and bitterness swept over me as I blamed my parents for not warning me, or preparing me for such encounters with men. Innocently I had trusted and walked blindly into situations which could have ruined, or ended my life. I stood crying against the door, pleading with the man to leave me alone. 'I am a Polish refugee and have been an internee of the German army. It is better that you don't come near me!' I cried. I had not lied. It was the truth. I had been an internee, but I hoped that he might put a false interpretation on my words and leave me alone, and he did! Nevertheless, I stood all night watching him, ready to defend myself should he approach me.

Early next morning, before his family were about, he unlocked the door and directed me towards the city. Such terrifying and abhorrent experiences seemed repeatedly to confront me and I feared for the time when I would not escape. I knew I had to be on my guard from now on. I had gone through the trauma of being trapped and confronted by evil intent, but God had saved me and I remained unharmed. I could now understand the horrors that women suffered during the war. I could feel their terror and understand the victims better.

With a sense of relief I entered the British Embassy. After so much suffering, I had at last arrived at the place which I believed would welcome me with open arms. At last I could see the way ahead to serve God.

I walked in confident and happy and put my case to a receptionist. Without being granted an interview I was rejected! One look at me, a displaced person, a penniless refugee and shabbily dressed, who could care. It taught me that no matter how repulsive or badly dressed a person looks to remember that he or she is a human being with feelings; and to look beyond what I see into the soul.

But the conviction that Britain was the place where God would lead me into full-time service continued to nag me.

There were camps for displaced persons, but I was hesitant to go for I still suffered from the trauma of the German labour camps. Displaced persons' camps were considered to be unsafe for girls on their own. With nothing to fill their time or minds, with no hope and shortage of food liaisons between men and women became an accepted way of life.

I returned from Hamburg discouraged and depressed. It was good to be home and help Mama and Papa but I remained unfulfilled. Cousin Paul wanted me back at the workshop. I had reached a crossroads and whatever I did, stay with my parents or return to the shoe factory, neither was leading to the full-time service which I craved. There was a Displaced Persons' camp in Westerstede, and I finally realised that there was no other way but to go there.

The camp was temporary and without proper facilities. I had no mattress or pillow when I arrived and slept rolled in a blanket on the wire mesh of an iron bedstead. I had endured worse and if it brought me nearer to God's service this did not matter. There were regular meals which were sufficient to keep hunger at bay. Everything was provided and in time I was given a mattress and pillow.

The atmosphere of the camp was, on the whole, congenial. We were all equal – we had nothing, only a desire to reach Britain for a better life. I attended English lessons which were given twice a week. Before I entered the camp I had bought with the wages from Paul material for a dress, coffee and an English/German dictionary.

We were free to come and go, but few risked leaving the camp because of the possibility of missing their transfer to Britain. Everyone was in a state of tension, waiting to hear that they had been accepted and had passage on a boat to England. Rumours raged, filling us with either hope or foreboding. I lived in perpetual fear that something would prevent me from reaching England. It was rumoured that we had to pay £10 for the boat fare, an amount far beyond my means. English money could only be obtained on the black market, and I had spent one thousand German marks (several months wages) just to buy the dress material, the coffee and the dictionary. (The dictionary, cheap and yellowed, is still one of my proudest possessions.)

My hopes rose and sank several times a day. Studying the English language and endeavouring to learn twenty new words each day was my calming therapy. I worked in a room from morning until lunchtime. In the afternoon I took piano lessons.

At last the news I eagerly awaited arrived. I was accepted, and because my cousins and Eugene had served in the Polish forces, I was granted a free passage.

In my usual optimistic manner, I believed that everything would be wonderful, indeed glorious! There had been talk of upholstered seats on trains and boat cabins. Reality was again contrary to my romantic notions. The train was crowded and uncomfortable. The boat was cold and draughty. Most of us were seasick. We slid to and fro on wooden benches and sighed with great relief when we berthed. But all the discomfort could not diminish our excitement that at last we were on British soil. At last we could begin a new life in a Christian country that was at peace!

7

Oh, to be in England!
Summer, 1947

God keeps faithful ...

The covered truck taking us to a transit camp prevented us from seeing the countryside or the people. I was buoyant and impatient to arrive at our destination in Gloucestershire. The excitement dissipated into weariness, however, when the first thing we did at the camp was to join a lengthy queue to have our documents checked. Two girls in army uniform coped with great difficulty. They had no knowledge of the Polish language and found spelling our names, and understanding us a problem. A Polish army officer stood by to assist, but one person liaising between two examiners did little to speed up the process. The queue continued to a store room where we were issued with bedding and then we were escorted to our living quarters in Nissen huts. The camp had previously been a military hospital and was well planned and provided good amenities.

The simple act of making my bed with clean white sheets and pillowcases was therapeutic. I felt less tense. The hut's interior was brightly painted and the sun shone through the curtained windows. In the middle of the room, standing on a concrete base, was an iron stove.

It was lit and the smell of the burning wood reminded me of my home in Poland. Everything was too novel for me to feel homesick and the kind reception made me feel safe.

As soon as I could I made my way to the tiny chapel and gave a prayer of thanksgiving. God had never deserted me. He had not prevented my suffering, but he had kept me in his loving care. Now it was up to me to fulfil my calling!

For some time I remained within the camp grounds not daring to venture out. The camp was situated in open countryside near the town of Cirencester. Except for traffic passing on a nearby road, and a few people walking their dogs, we saw no-one.

Passing the camp telephone box I had a strong urge to go in. I resisted. It seemed a foolish impulse. I knew no-one in Britain. The feeling, however, did not leave me. Next time I was near the telephone kiosk I walked towards it – then retreated. What if someone saw me and asked who I was 'phoning? I had no names or addresses. Days passed and still something was prompting me to go to the telephone box. I could resist it no longer and went in.

Flicking through the directory my eyes fell on a page with entries of 'The Salvation Army'. I believed in salvation! Surely, whatever this organisation was, it must also believe in salvation, otherwise why be called by that name. I was still puzzled and apprehensive but decided, then and there, to copy down the name and address of the first one on the list.

I wrote saying that I was a Polish refugee, a Christian, and that I was seeking Christian fellowship. To my surprise, I received a reply by return of post giving me information about the Salvation Army Corps in Cirencester, and dates and times of meetings.

The next Sunday, after lunch, I walked into Cirencester. I was nervous. It was my first step out of the camp and I did not know what to expect or if it was safe walking alone. England was totally unknown to me and I knew so little of the language that I had difficulty understanding the English-speaking people and they had difficulty understanding me.

Cirencester was a quiet, pleasant place – really beautiful with its ancient buildings and cathedral. The shops had lovely displays of beautiful clothes and some were stocked with food such as I had never seen before. I was happy and at ease. There were a few people, who either gazed in shop windows or walked at a leisurely pace. I felt safe.

After asking several people the way to the Salvation Army Hall I found it by following their pointing fingers, rather than their explanations. The hall was situated in a quiet road at the other end of the town and I recognised it by its sign 'The Salvation Army'. Children were playing on the surrounding wall. As I approached a rather stout lady came out chastising the children. I cowered away, now unsure of entering the hall. When she had gone back into the hall, I asked the children, 'What is going on in this hall?' They replied, 'It is for soldiers!'

The word 'soldier' startled me. I decided to wait. If soldiers were going in I would take off! I really could not endure any more military personnel! The stout lady came out again. Seeing me hovering about she approached me and invited me into the hall, explaining that the meeting was for children, but I could see the Captain. At the word 'captain' I froze, and wanted to run away. This was even worse, for surely no army captain would teach a children's Sunday School! A slim young woman came out and the stout woman pointed to her saying, 'Here she is. This is Captain Evans!' I was more confused than ever!

The Captain invited me in, saying, 'We are about to begin a children's Sunday School and then we have a meeting for the grown-ups with tea afterwards. Do come in and stay for tea!' The word 'tea' persuaded me and I went in.

There were a number of German prisoners-of-war at the adults' meeting. The service had been especially planned for them. Through my knowledge of German I was able to talk with them, whilst we ate the sandwiches and home-made cakes.

Captain Alice Evans invited me to her quarters and during tea I plied her with questions as best I could in my broken English. I asked her if she was an ordained minister?; how did she acquire her qualifications?; how much did it cost to go to college? She told me that she had been ordained after training at the Salvation Army International Training College. There were no fees to pay.

I grew animated as I listened. If the training was free, this was the way for me, for I had no money or financial support. I was excited. I wanted to train immediately. It took the Captain great effort to calm me down and explain that I had to become a Salvation Army soldier (member) first. After initial training and interviews I had to be accepted as a candidate and then pass a preliminary examination to qualify as a student.

In my enthusiasm I had not considered what I would need; for instance, a number of books for study, a Salvation Army outfit – uniform, shoes, bonnet, etc. The words of Revelation 3:7 sprang into my mind. 'I have set before you an open door and no man can shut it!' I saw the open door and nothing was going to close it against me!

The open door?

It was November and I made up my mind to enter college the following August – the beginning of the college year. I had given myself only eight months to do so!

My earnestness was contagious and Captain Evans used her influence to speed up my candidature. Without her trust and backing I would never have made it. The devil seemed determined to frustrate my efforts, and when things went wrong, as so often they did, I became very depressed. My reason for coming to Britain was to be ordained or a missionary and I was determined to succeed.

During this time I was under pressure by the camp authorities to take a job or leave. I had registered for work in a chocolate factory, or domestic service – the only choices open to women immigrants. Once accepted for employment I was bound by a contract to remain for at least two years. I was afraid that this would prevent me from going to the Salvation Army college.

Meanwhile, Alice Evans, becoming lonely living on her own, had applied to the Divisional Commander for a second officer. Her application was accepted and the post of Candidate helper was offered to me. This was wonderful news. However, there were still many obstacles to overcome before I could take up the post.

The British army Major, in charge of the camp, invited me to his home over the Christmas period to help his wife. I did the housework and I learned how to use a vacuum cleaner and washing machine for the first time. It was a beautiful home. I had an insight into the English way of life and was treated well. I worked for two weeks and as well as receiving my board and lodgings I was paid £2. The Major and his wife tried to persuade me to work for them. I knew that not only would this employment prevent me from entering college, but I was on duty from early morning until late at night with little free time and little opportunity to study.

And I overheard the Major and his wife talking.

The wife asked, 'Have you registered Janina, yet?'

The Major replied, 'Before she can be registered as a maid, she must work for at least a month.'

I was taken aback. The fact that they were trying to register me without my knowledge appalled and frightened me. I felt trapped and gave every possible excuse to leave.

This experience taught me to be on my guard and tell no-one about my plans. When I returned to camp the Major continued to put pressure on me to work for his wife. I was unable to refuse every request, but when I did consent I worked for no more than a few days at a time. I had a comfortable well-furnished room. The family trusted me to be in the house alone. The wife even took me visiting and shopping for she liked my company.

Only the grown-up daughter, who was a day pupil at a local college, looked down on me. My shabby appearance possibly contributed to this attitude. On one occasion I was asked to change before lunch. There were no visitors, only the wife and daughter at home, and I felt it unreasonable to be asked to wear my only dress – a silk one Mama had given me and which was kept for church – to serve a meal and wash up.

Without warning we were told that all displaced persons were being transferred to another camp. The Polish Staff Officer had befriended me and employed me to help him with his administrative work. He had encouraged me to type and act as an interpreter. Miraculously, it seemed, because of these duties I was one of the few who remained. I thanked God, for by remaining in Cirencester I was able to wait for confirmation of my appointment to the Salvation Army.

My relief changed to consternation when the Polish officer, Henryk, told me that the reason I was not transferred or forced to take employment was because he had informed the authorities that we were being married and that I was his office assistant. He hastily explained, 'I know that I am a Catholic and that you are a Protestant, but I don't mind! I won't even object to you joining the Salvation Army and going to college, as long as we are married sometime!' I was aghast! I tried to explain that I would not be accepted into the Salvation Army Training college if I was engaged unless my fiancé was also a Salvationist. Henryk was undeterred, and determined to marry me.

The Major, meanwhile, was doing his utmost to register me as his maid. I didn't know which was the worse dilemma, but I knew somehow I had to escape.

My few belongings were kept under my bed in a wooden box. I now kept it packed, so that the instant I heard from the Salvation Army I could make a bolt for it. The days dragged by and I could scarcely bear the tension. I had no-one to whom I could turn, and I knew I could be detained in the camp by force until I was registered in employment. There was only the Polish officer's word against mine, and he had a friend keeping a close watch on me. I dared not admit to the English Major that it wasn't true that Henryk and I were being married, for he would have exerted more pressure on me to become his housemaid.

In time, the letter arrived from the Salvation Army informing me that I had been accepted. I wanted to shout and jump for joy. Waiting until everyone was asleep I stole out of the camp carrying all my belongings and reached the Salvation Army Captain's house well past midnight. Alice was surprised, but pleased to see me. Next morning we wasted no time in completing all the necessary registration documents to make certain that no-one could prevent me from leaving the transit camp.

It was mandatory that I wear a Salvation Army uniform, but I had no means to purchase one. I bought black dye and dyed my stockings and shoes. I was given an old bonnet, a well worn out-of-date pleated jacket and torn skirt (both of different materials) from members. Using an old broken hand-sewing machine, I endeavoured to reshape the tunic and skirt into a wearable uniform.

Before many days had passed, my whereabouts were discovered by the camp authorities, and my peace was shattered. The English Major came and gave me a severe reprimand. He would ignore my hurried unofficial departure if I agreed to become his maid.

Henryk was distraught. His plans to marry me appeared hopeless but he would not give in. He continued to give me work as an interpreter and called frequently at our quarters. I tried to hide, but he was so charming and well mannered that Alice could not resist inviting him in. He brought us both presents. Henryk's knowledge of English was very poor and he could not understand the Captain. I watched with amusement as they tried to communicate with each other, knowing that Henryk was trying to befriend Alice in order to gain her support to persuade me to marry him.

I was becoming more and more involved in the Salvation Army work. I took a Sunday School class which was quite hilarious at times for I understood the children's accent less than I did the adults. In my home-made uniform I sat beside the Captain at the front facing the members. Eventually I was asked to give my first sermon. The German prisoners-of-war still attended the meetings, and as they understood little English I chose to deliver my address in German. It also made the task much easier for me.

I took as my text 1 Corinthians 15 – the Resurrection of Christ. I explained how Paul, before he was converted, had persecuted the Christians, and that he died a martyr for his faith and belief in the resurrection. I was so carried away that I spoke for twenty minutes. The English congregation, who could not understand a word I said, sat still and quiet. I had hardly finished, when four Germans came forward and knelt at the mercy seat. The

Captain asked me to pray for them.

This was my first experience of ministering and I took it as a sign of God's approval. I was now certain that I was on the right path. If I kept faith, God would help me overcome all obstacles.

The Divisional Commander and the Divisional Youth Secretary attended meetings which I conducted, to assess my progress. I sat and passed the preliminary examinations, and then concentrated on my sermons and studies for the final examinations.

Captain Evans was indeed a true servant of Christ. She was kind, loving, patient, and she taught me well. She was, also, a faithful companion and mother figure. We shared the self-denial collections, cycling the many miles around the scattered Gloucestershire villages; stood in the streets in all kinds of weather on flag days; calling at public houses and selling the *War Cry* and *Young Soldier* newspapers. We visited the sick, and baby-sat to give tired mothers a rest. Whatever we did God seemed to bless our efforts.

To help me save for my college outfit and send food parcels to my family in Germany, our food was kept very simple. Lettuce sandwiches were our staple diet in summer. I was so absorbed in my own ambitions that I failed to realise how much this scrimping meant to Alice, who was used to a better diet. Our accommodation was very old and draughty, and yet we economised on heating as well, huddling around a small fireplace for warmth.

The members of the Corps were kind and supportive. Coupons were still needed to buy clothing and few were issued to each person. Members gave me coupons so that I could obtain underclothing and a dressing-gown. I was compelled to make a promise in writing to the Divisional Commander that I would have all the clothing and uniform required for the commencement of the college year. This meant that I had to buy most of my clothes second-hand.

At the candidates' interview we had to answer (on paper) many questions, including: Where do you keep your money? a) A bank. b) Under the mattress. I wrote down, 'Neither. I have no money.' When interviewed and asked to explain this answer, the National Candidates Secretary could not comprehend how anyone could want to train at college and yet have no money. A member of the panel, Major Newall said, 'What faith. She believes that God, who helped her so far, will continue to do so. How wonderful!' When asked how I paid my train fare to London for the interview, I explained that I had been in London acting as an interpreter and this work paid for my fare.

When the Divisional Commander realised that I had no income or savings, he suggested that I work in the Salvation Army Red Shield canteens, but I felt that this would only hinder my studies. Doubts of entering college began to worry me. I had nine sets of monthly lessons to be completed in half the time. The D.C. became reluctant to speed up my candidature. His reason was that I had only recently been enrolled as a soldier and had hardly any clothing, never mind a uniform. He had advised the Captain to put me on a three months probationary period before deciding I was fit to become a candidate, but she had refused.

The Divisional Commander continued to argue,

'Pladek,' he said, 'is a foreigner who has only been in this country a few months. She is a complete stranger to us with little knowledge of English. I have to explain everything with great difficulty and am unable to get a coherent answer!' He turned to me saying, 'Cirencester is a very small Corps. You have no experience of any other. Some of the Corps members have been here all their lives. What could you teach them, or preach to them? All you know is what you have seen or heard at a few meetings!'

I replied, 'Sir, the Salvation army believes in the Bible and the Word of God revealed in it. So do I. All I shall ever attempt to tell the people is the Word of God.' He did not answer, and this gave me courage. I continued, 'Sir, I know I need to improve my English. To continue being an interpreter for the transit camp whenever I can will benefit me more than working in a canteen!' Captain Evans stubbornly defended me. She advised me, however, to conquer my shyness and discourage Henryk.

During a junior legion meeting in our home, when we were teaching children home crafts, the English Major arrived. We were polishing brass. When he saw what I was doing, he remarked coldly, 'What sort of a life do you wish to commit yourself to? This? Look at yourself! Compared to my home what is this?' He looked around the poorly furnished room, and at my grubby hands and continued. 'I tell you to change your mind now!' He was angry, frustrated and paced up and down. I ignored him and finally, still fuming, he left.

I continued to study well into the night and my efforts were rewarded. I passed all my examinations and in time received confirmation of my acceptance to college. To help me raise enough money for my uniform the Divisional Peoples' secretary arranged a special meeting in Bristol. I was to be guest speaker and beneficiary of a special collection. I was well received. The members were generous and I also received the gift of a suitcase, work overalls and a bonnet. A young khaki-clad British army corporal gave the final prayers, and I was impressed by his sincerity.

With the money I purchased a boys' dressing-gown as it was the cheapest. I needed an umbrella and when a tinker came offering me one for ten shillings, I eagerly bought it. The Captain was out at the time, but when she returned, she took one look at the umbrella and re-marked, 'You've been done! There is a church jumble sale today. We will go there now. It is a bit late, but there are sure to be bargains, and sometimes they are reduced towards the end of the day.' We each paid sixpence for admission. There was very little left at the sale – and no reductions! I needed shoes and tried on a pair of black suede ones. They fitted badly and hurt, but they were black and I needed them to complete my uniform for college. I paid five shillings and I soon knew that 'I was done'.

Training college
August arrived and the day I left for college. It was a proud moment for Captain Evans, and I vowed not to let her down.

I travelled by train to London from Bristol Templemeads where I joined other cadets. They were animated and talked aloud about their feelings. This was the realisation of their ambitions to enter the International Training College and hopefully once commissioned to serve God anywhere in the world.

During the journey I sat opposite the young corporal who had led the prayers at my 'benefit' meeting. He introduced himself as Douglas Neale and his companion, Douglas Hilborne, who sat beside me. I knew no-one and was too overwhelmed to speak. I sat withdrawn, but listened with interest to the others. When we arrived in London someone suggested a taxi. I was taken aback, but need not have worried for Douglas Neale paid the fare. He grabbed my suitcase and off we went. I felt comforted. Someone cared. I was not alone after all.

When we arrived at Denmark Hill and I had my first glimpse of the college building, the statues of William and Catherine Booth, the magnificent tower and grounds, the staircase leading to the entrance where officers stood waiting to welcome us, I was overcome and burst into tears. At last, I was at the beginning of full-time service for God.

Standing in the reception hall the sense of loneliness, which had surfaced throughout my life, welled up within me. I felt a complete stranger. The other cadets all appeared to know someone and greeted each other with excitement and affection. I knew no-one, and stood apart and looked on. I had arrived, but understood and spoke very little English. Making friends would not be easy. I was consoled, however, in the knowledge that we all shared the desire to serve God, and that he would unite us.

I concentrated on my studies, not only during the lectures and study hours, but in the evenings and most of our free half days. For a treat I sometimes took a tram ride to a shopping centre and bought an iced bun.

The college clothing list which was sent to me, I found to my shame and embarrassment, was out of date. My clothes were too long. I had thick black stockings instead of fine rayon ones which the other women cadets wore. I had followed implicitly the instructions and purchased all the items listed. The other cadets had a more casual attitude to authority. I was the only one who had bought every item of equipment. The others shrugged their shoulders and said, 'There are no strict rules. A promise to buy the item later is sufficient!'

My uniform was not only second-hand but was old-fashioned. The tunic buttoned to the neck with bone buttons. The other cadets had the modern style; open front jacket with the Salvation Army crest on blue or red silk blouse fronts and matching buttons. The overseas cadets from Sweden, Denmark, Norway, Switzerland, Finland and Brazil were particularly well dressed. Their uniforms were tailored in expensive cloth, with red or maroon trimmings which emphasised the chic design. By comparison I was a poor sight, standing out like a sore thumb and I knew it.

A Swedish cadet voiced the opinion of the others. 'Pladek,' she said, 'Do you realise that you are a disgrace to the cadets?' She looked me up and down, making me more conscious of my old-fashioned uniform, badly fitting second-hand shoes and thick stockings! I tried to explain my situation and she listened. When I had finished, she retorted, 'That is a tall story! How could you manage to enter college straight from a Displaced Persons' camp and not have a relative to help you?' Her unkindness and insensitivity hurt me deeply, but not as much as being thought a liar. However, as the months passed and the cadets heard my testimony their attitude changed considerably and I became happily integrated into college life.

The college curriculum consisted of study, work sessions, prayer and quarterly examinations. In addition, we helped at Corps meetings, undertook door-to-door collections, visitations, Open-air meetings and Joy hours. We marched through London and sang in the street, markets and Underground stations. We organised special events and sold admission tickets. All the time we were supervised by the House officers and cadet sergeants.

I worked conscientiously and always sold my ticket allocation, but was hurt when I began to be taken for granted. A few cadets felt it difficult or demeaning to sell tickets in shops, etc. and brought them back. I would return pleased with my efforts having sold them all, but tired and in need of a rest. The sergeant seemed to wait for me and called out, 'Oh, Pladek, you are good at selling tickets. Go out and sell these, too! You will won't you. Thanks.' On one occasion I had to refuse. I was reluctant to do so, but my shoes had crippled my feet and I felt I could not walk another step. Afterwards, when the pain had eased, I felt ashamed at my refusal. Perhaps I was more experienced at selling than the others, for I had had plenty of practice in Poland when Mama sent me out to sell flowers, lettuce and rhubarb at street corners.

Taking all things into consideration, however, the spirit and fellowship of the college was good. I am certain that if the women had really understood my circumstances, and the difficulty I had adjusting after the trauma of my wartime experiences, they would have had more compassion. One or two invited me to join them on their half-day trips into London, but I had to refuse on the grounds that I could not afford it. They would shrug their shoulders and say, 'What is a few shillings, or a pound. Surely you can afford that!' I was left alone, feeling inadequate, misunderstood and hurt! In some ways, quite unintentionally, they made me feel an outcast.

When I left for college the Corps members had a collection for me, for I had saved nothing from my allowance. When I had paid my share of the food, light and fuel bills, and my contribution to the Corps, I had less that two shillings left. This went towards my clothes and a food parcel to my family who were still in poor circumstances.

The gift of money provided me with the books I needed. When a Book Sale was held I bought as many as I could at half-price. This left me almost penniless.

It was part of the cadet training to assist with the national Salvation Army annual Self-Denial week – a project that took place each February, and covered the whole of Great Britain. The college received a percentage of the funds raised. To encourage the cadets to do well, the one raising the most money was officially acknowledged.

I was totally dependent on the college and to repay it I was determined to achieve, or surpass, the previous year's target. Each cadet was assigned to a Corps. I was appointed to Stockport in Cheshire. Unfortunately I was taken ill and confined to the college sick bay. The nursing sister advised me to remain in college and convalesce, but I was anxious to take part in the collection. I persuaded her to give me permission to leave for Stockport. Three days after the other cadets had left, I travelled by train, the college paying for my fare.

Because the district I had to cover was extensive and some distance from the officers' quarters, the Major in charge suggested that I travel by bus or tram. I could claim reimbursement of the fares on production of the used tickets. I was taken aback as I had no money. In my embarrassment I whispered, 'I have no money!' The Major straightened his back and gave me a withering look which said, 'I don't believe you!' Dismissing me he said, 'Then you'll have to walk to and from the district!'

No one ever believed me when I confessed that I had no money, not even when in obvious embarrassment I would whisper, 'I have no money.'

'How could anyone plan to go to college without a penny!' was the stock reply.

I trudged the streets of Stockport. My feet hurt and, whenever I could, I walked in my bare feet slipping my shoes back on when I saw anyone approaching. Waiting until they were out of sight I took them off again. I collected from early morning until late at night; in the dark, the rain and cold, often walking in my stockinged feet. In spite of my weak condition, my painful feet, I finished my collection and surpassed the previous year's target! I returned to college with a sense of deep satisfaction.

Douglas

A cadet, called Brenda, befriended me. She was dark, attractive and had a lovely soprano voice. I admired her and valued her friendship.

One day she came to me and said, 'Pladek, there is a boy in love with you! Aren't you bothered?'

I did not believe her.

She continued, 'He is nice and likeable. He plays the solo cornet in the cadets' band.'

I wanted to believe it was Douglas Neale, but thinking it was his friend, Douglas Hilborne, I replied, 'I am certain he is not in love with me!'

Brenda persisted and said, 'It is obvious to me that Douglas likes you! I wish it was me.'

I began to observe the two men and soon realised that Brenda was right. Douglas Neale was interested in me, and his friend Douglas was only befriending me. Douglas Neale often stood watching the entrance to the women cadets' quarters and when he saw me he would walk towards me and make polite conversation. Just seeing Douglas made me glow inside, but I was determined to observe the strict rule and not contemplate any serious relationships until after I had been commissioned for at least one year.

At the end of the course and prior to being commissioned the college issued us with a new lieutenant's uniform. There were two types of uniform. One provided free. The other, for which we had to contribute £1, was made of a better quality serge cloth. It was obviously more prudent to pay £1, for the uniform looked smarter and would last longer. We were encouraged to order it.

Joan, my closest friend, tried to persuade me to pay the pound. She urged, 'Look, Pladek. It's only £1! Surely you have got that much! You are very silly not to take advantage of the offer!'

In truth, I did not have enough money. I had bought maroon felt trimming in Woolworth's for one shilling to improve the epaulettes of my old uniform, and after paying the tram fare, I had only one shilling and sixpence left. I was, therefore, short of eighteen shillings and sixpence.

I explained to Joan, 'I do not have enough to have my shoes heeled. It costs two shillings and sixpence for the poorest heels, but if I explain to the shoe repairer, I am hoping he will do me a favour for one shilling and sixpence!'

Joan stood mouth open and then said, 'Pladek, I just can't believe you!'

The shoe repairer did, however, and I had my shoes mended for one shilling and sixpence.

The day arrived when we received our lieutenant's uniform. I was the only student with the free one. Joan was right. The outfit was made of poor material and did not fit or hang well. Looking at the other girls I felt like the ugly duckling. When I was asked to report to the college administrator I quite expected to be told that I had let the college down. Imagine my joy and surprise when I was told that my Divisional Headquarters had offered to buy me a tailored uniform for my commissioning. I was ecstatic and hurried off to be measured. The outfit was made in the best quality material and I proudly wore it for many years. Many times I wondered how my HQ knew of my dilemma!

We had some leisure time at the end of the college year. Douglas Neale became my constant companion and we grew fond of each other. When we walked together I was conscious and proud of the admiring glances we received. The House Officer approached us when we were standing in a group. She scrutinised me closely, and remarked, 'Well, well, Pladek, what a transformation! Clothes certainly make people!' I smiled and thanked her, but her implication that I was different in fine clothes bothered me. My appearance had changed, and certainly gave me more confidence, but in my heart I hoped that I was the same person.

We were commissioned with great pageantry in the Royal Albert Hall. It was May 1949. Douglas' parents came and after the ceremony he took me to meet them. I knew then that he was serious about our relationship.

Next day we were given our appointments. Douglas was posted to Belfast and I to Fife, Scotland.

I boarded the train at King's Cross Station, London. As it steamed out of the station I sat back. I was pulsating with a new energy and anxious to begin my life serving God.

The movement of the train soothed me and I began to daydream. I was now on my spiritual journey and had a destination. I was now a woman – 23 years old and ordained. I had broken through the suffering and degradation of my wartime childhood years and emerged, like a butterfly, into a new world which promised better times. The rhythm of the wheels began to echo in my head. I was compelled to listen.

Suddenly I sat up. Were they telling me something? Aa-fri-caa; aa-fri-caa; aa-fri-caa ... Africa!! The voice which spoke to me in the orchard in Poland was speaking to me now! I panicked! Why, if I was meant to serve God in Africa was I going north to Scotland, a country unknown to me? Then, like a great amen, the words from Habakkuk 2: 2 filled my mind – 'It is not yet time for it to come true. But what I show you will come true. It may seem slow but wait for it. It will certainly take place; and will not be delayed.'

I had to learn patience and accept his will, for that time was yet to be ....

APPENDIX

Further milestones

1949: Janina was commissioned into the Salvation Army and took up here first command in Dundee, Scotland. Her service and work in the community with young street youths and alcoholics attracted the attention of the press. *The Daily Record* carried a daily feature on her work for a whole week.

1950: Janina married Douglas Neale, a Salvation Army lieutenant whom she had met at the Training College when they were both cadets.

1950-1976: Served in many parts of Scotland i.e. Kinlochleven, Argyll, Glasgow, Thurso, Dundee, Dumbarton, Edinburgh and Paisley.

1961-1976: The Neales were Divisional Youth secretaries, serving the whole of Scotland. During this time they became widely known both within and without the Salvation Army, especially for their national youth camps, holiday schools and highly successful productions of modern Christian musicals. Janina was the principal initiator, co-ordinator, producer and business manager of the shows. Janina was appointed Divisional Guide Commissioner.

1976: The Neale's were transferred to South Africa and were appointed Divisional Commanders with the responsibility to oversee the work in Johannesburg, Pretoria, the whole of the Transvaal, Durban and large areas of Natal/Kwa-Zulu land.

1976-1985: In Zululand with responsibility for eight major Childcare and community projects on behalf of the USA based 'World Vision' Charity. At any one time over 3,000 children were involved. The work included practical and spiritual aid, school feeding projects, clothing the needy, educational and scripture lessons. Community work involved providing and safeguarding water supplies; school buildings; adult literacy classes; sewing seminars; managing the mission far; visiting churches across the whole of Zululand – preaching virtually every day.

Their service earned them the commendation of Chief Minister Mangosutha Bethelezi and the Zulu King Goodwill Zwelethini and they were adopted as White Zulus.

It was a wonderful reunion when the Rev. Gerhardt, the German evangelist who visited Janina's home in Poland before the war, came to preach with her in Mountain View, South Africa. Gerhardt's son, a missionary in South America, accompanied him. Before the Gerhardts' left they financed a project to provide water for a village in Zululand.

1985: Based in Johannesburg, Bloemfontein, Kimberley and Lesotho. During this time they became aware of the thousands of homeless boys and unemployed men and youths who lived on the streets of Johannesburg and the surrounding towns and villages.

In addition to the official duties Janina began a 'foodrun' for them. She left home before 7 am and returned at 7 pm and moved among the hundreds of black poor alone.

The principal Johannesburg newspaper, *Star* carried a feature on her naming her 'Mother Theresa of South Africa'.

Now officially retired and living in Aberdeen the Neales return to South Africa where they keep in touch with many of the townsfolk they helped. Recently they took musical instruments and clothing to Mozambique and conducted Easter services in the Ciskei.

They were invited into Mandela's township, where they preached and had 38 converts. They risked their lives in doing so. The Neales are still highly esteemed in South Africa. When in this country they are frequently invited to preach in interdenominational churches throughout Great Britain.

Update:
Janina's wartime ordeal impaired her health. On her recent return from a visit to her daughter Christina and family she suffered a severe heart attack whilst on a flight to Boston. Her life was saved by the prompt action of two doctors who were also passengers to Boston and on their way to the Massachusetts General Hospital – a hospital renowned worldwide for its heart surgery. Janina was taken there and after weeks of intensive care was able to fly back to her home in Aberdeen. Although forced to adopt a less strenuous lifestyle, Janina continues to serve the Lord by correspondence. Douglas has an arthritic condition but travels and preaches throughout Scotland. The poor in Africa are not forgotten. Regular parcels are sent to the poor and to the homeless.

The Pladek Family

The grandparents of Janina Neale were Joseph (born 1864) who married Karina (born 1867). Joseph was born in Czechoslovakia, then farmed in the Ukraine but settled with Karina in Poland after the First World War when communism spread through Russia. The land he obtained, however, was too poor to farm and he made a living as a miller and baker. Their children were Janina (born 1896) and Emanuel Joseph (born 1897)

Janina was educated at the University of Budapest, then practised as a dental surgeon in the Ukraine. She was tortured to death by the communists when only 24-years-old for her Christian faith and loyalty to her parents. She had refused to co-operate with the communists and spy on her patients.

Emanuel Joseph was educated at the University of Budapest. After only one year when he had gained distinction in several languages, the First World War broke out and he was conscripted into the Russian Army and served as an officer. Captured by the Germans in 1916 he spent the rest of the war in a prisoner of war camp, returning to the Ukraine crippled with arthritis. His Christian faith had deepened and he became an evangelical preacher travelling from village to village, often sleeping on benches or railway carriages.

Emanuel Joseph married Paulina

Paulina Yelets was born in the Ukraine in a remote village too far from a school, so she was deprived of a formal education. When she met and married Joseph he taught her to read and write. She was a warm, affectionate person, totally committed to her husband's evangelism.

When his mission became too difficult and dangerous under the communist regime, the Pladeks left the Ukraine and settled in Poland with Joseph's parents in the village of Judrowice, near the city of Lodz. Janina was born in 1926, Gienek in 1927, Felix in 1930, and Theodore in 1939.

What happened to Janina's family?

Eugene was compelled to return to Scotland with the Polish forces for his demobilisation. He never returned to Germany. After staying some time in Scotland, long enough to visit Janina in the Displaced Persons' camp at Cirencester, he emigrated to Argentina. Eugene developed his skills as a builder and became successful. He married and had two sons. Sadly the firstborn died in infancy. Janina and Douglas visited Eugene in 1977 at his home in Buenos Aires, but it was not until 1994 that he was reunited with his brother Felix, when Felix, too, made the journey to see him.

Felix married but remained in Westerstede in a flat near his parents. In 1993 he revisited the family home in Poland, taking his eldest son with him. The ordeal was too much for Felix and he suffered a nervous breakdown on his return.

Theo won a scholarship to the University of Hieldelburg and attained every degree in Theology. He married and is now a lecturer in Theology at Munster University.

Mama and Papa

Joseph's health continued to deteriorate and he became more disabled. When Felix left home he was unable to undertake the farm work and fulfil the duties required to stay in the barn accommodation. Mark, the Baptist minister, came to their aid. In exchange for looking after the church buildings they were allowed to occupy the barn accommodation which annexed the church. As was the custom in that part of rural Germany, cows and pigs were also housed in the barn.

Paulina, however, was a shrewd business woman and was determined to improve their circumstances. She grew flowers and vegetables in the small piece of land surrounding the barn, and sold them. In time the Pladeks bought cheaply a dilapidated barn and moved into it. The authorities were appalled at the condition of the property and immediately condemned it as unfit for human habitation. The villagers, impressed by the pluck of the elderly couple, rallied to help them and soon the barn was considered fit to live in. Joseph and Paulina continued to improve the property and land. Paulina cultivated the half acre and realised a cherished dream when she planted cherry trees and harvested the fruit – just as she had done in Poland!

Joseph died in 1959 but not before he, too, had realised a deep longing. Douglas and Janina motored to Germany and brought the parents to Scotland. Whilst there Joseph was able to hear his beloved daughter proclaim the love of God as she preached and converted members of her faith. Sadly he died a month after he returned home. Paulina died peacefully in 1975.

Short history of Poland

The Pladek children grew up in a troubled but proud country. Poland was struggling from the aftermath of the 1914-1918 war, but with astonishing patriotic zeal rose, phoenix-like, to become recognised as an independent state, a status returned to her by the Treaty of Versailles in 1919.

Until 1772 Poland was a huge country. It was, however, a very weak one. Situated on the great European plain it did not have natural defences, such as high mountain ranges provide, to protect itself against aggressive neighbours. It had a feeble system of government. Its king was elected by nobles. The nobles were selfish and greedy and were easily bribed by the three neighbouring states, Russian, Prussia (Germany) and Austria, who paid well for their allegiance and votes.

Russia, Prussia and Austria were rivals of each other, all wanting more territory for themselves and afraid that the others would gain too much. As a result of this corruption and aggression Poland disappeared from the map when it was divided among the three powers in 1772, 1793 and 1795. A Duchy of Warsaw was set up by Napoleon but vanished with his defeat, and the signing of the Treaty of Vienna in 1815.

Polish nationalism did not die, however, and was particularly active in Russian Poland where there was a ruthless suppression of the most basic rights of the people. A revolt by the Poles in 1830 led to the rebels being hung or shot. Thousands were exiled to the saltmines of Siberia or remote parts of Russia. Estates were confiscated and sold to Russian families; the Polish flag and language was banned. The Catholic church, the bulwark of Polish tradition, came under attack and its properties were seized. Further uprisings by the Poles in 1848 and 1863 were crushed with such brutal retribution by the three powers that British sympathy was aroused and it tried to intervene. This concern, however, sadly dwindled into indifference.

In 1869 Russia made the Russian language and education policies compulsory, and Polish schools were closed. As a result there were fewer schools in Poland in 1919 than there had been in the 14th century.

Heavy penalties were inflicted on persons evading the law.

Barred from government office or public service, the Poles turned their energies to commerce, and Warsaw and Lodz became thriving cities. Mines were opened, and but for the fact that the Poles were forbidden by their oppressors to build roads and bridges, Poland could have become a well developed commercial state. From this bitter oppression, however, there emerged a strong nationalistic people, freedom loving, proud and courageous.

The 1914-18 war raged over the length and breadth of Poland destroying nearly two million homes and farms. Industrial plants were destroyed and the country emerged from the war completely ruined and systemically plundered. The war, however, provided the opportunity for Poland to be re-created by the Treaty of Versailles in 1919.

The treaty did not recognise Poland's right to compensation and rebuilding a nation without foreign aid seemed beyond the powers of the hapless people. Poland had to clear away the destruction of its cities, towns, and start to rebuild factories, hospitals, schools, bridges and roads. Without factories there was no employment, and Polish existence became dependent on a primitive form of agriculture. Farms divided into small holdings provided an inadequate living.

The poor economy led to a seriously undernourished nation ravaged by epidemics of virulent diseases and viruses brought in by the thousands of refugees fleeing across Poland from communist Russia.

The war-damaged hospitals could not cope and 1,400 Russian refugees are reported to have died in Baranowicze alone.

The League of Nations, in an attempt to stop the rising tide of deaths and the spread of the diseases, such as typhoid, malaria, smallpox and tuberculosis donated £187,000, but many years were to pass before a vaccination programme was begun. Janina Pladek, in fact, received her first inoculation when 8 years old.

Hygienic and sanitary conditions were primitive in Poland. There was no drainage or water supply at the Pladek's farm. A dry lavatory was situated far from the house for health reasons and water was drawn from a well dug by the parents. A wooden bucket, suspended over the well on the thin pole was connected to a long heavy crossbar. The well was 'struck' by the Pladeks, and Janina recalls the great rejoicing when the water was found.

Health surveillance was carried out by members of the Polish Red Cross who visited schools. A check was kept by cards filled in by children stating how often they washed their hair, body, feet, etc.

Until his death in 1935 Marshal Pilsudski directed

the destinies of Poland when the country experienced a period of calm financial stability and astonishing economic prosperity. A ten year non-aggression pact had been signed with Germany in 1934 and there were cordial relations between the two countries. Poland was allied to Britain. Unrest between Germany and Czechoslovakia seemed unlikely to affect this nation!